April 2008

For Frank Nobiletti –
Best wishes,
Kim Marshall

the
great
SEX
Secret

the
great
SEX
Secret

*what satisfied women and men know
that no one talks about*

Kim Marshall

SOURCEBOOKS CASABLANCA™
AN IMPRINT OF SOURCEBOOKS, INC.®
NAPERVILLE, ILLINOIS

This book is not intended as a substitute for medical advice from a qualified physician. The intent of this book is to provide accurate general information in regard to the subject matter covered. If medical advice or other expert help is needed, the services of an appropriate medical professional should be sought.

Published by Sourcebooks Casablanca, an imprint of Sourcebooks, Inc.
P.O. Box 4410, Naperville, Illinois 60567-4410
(630) 961-3900
Fax: (630) 961-2168
www.sourcebooks.com

Library of Congress Cataloging-in-Publication Data

Marshall, Kim.
  The Great Sex Secret : what satisfied women and men know that no one talks about / Kim Marshall.
     p. cm.
  Includes bibliographical references.
  ISBN-13: 978-1-4022-0810-2
  ISBN-10: 1-4022-0810-3
  1. Sex. 2. Orgasm. I. Title.

HQ31.M335 2006
613.9'6--dc22
2006021552

Printed and bound in the United States of America
DR 10 9 8 7 6 5 4 3 2 1

To Rhoda, with love

Table of Contents

Acknowledgments...ix

Introduction 1

Chapter 1:
Disappointment in the Land of Eros:
  Is There a Design Flaw? 7

Chapter 2:
Wham, Bam, Thank You, Ma'am:
  The Long History of One-Sided Sex.......................27

Chapter 3:
No Female Orgasm—But He Tried...........................45

Chapter 4:
Faking It and Dealing with It 63

Chapter 5:
Simultaneous Orgasms: Are They Possible? 79

Chapter 6:
Three Approaches to Mutual Satisfaction 107

Chapter 7:
What's Technique Got to Do with It? 131

Chapter 8:
Keeping Passion Alive in Long-Term
    Relationships...155

Chapter 9:
Finding Our Way to Sexual Happiness 177

Bibliography 197

Endnotes..203

About the Author 213

Acknowledgments

The author wishes to thank an intrepid group of "critical friends" whose comments and support helped move this book from a twelve-page essay to what it is today. Without their patience, candor, and encouragement the book wouldn't exist. My heartfelt thanks to Rhoda Schneider, Lillie Marshall, David Marshall, Katherine Marshall, Jon Saphier, Ted Dooley, Andrew Bundy, Karen Hansen, Christina Ward, Carol Schneider, Peg Winship, Rick Weissbourd, Michael Sunog, Lauren Dunbar Keough, Dick Keough, Roland Barth, John Dempsey, Barney Brawer, Jim Cutler, Don Cutler, Jill Kneerim, Paul Zofnass, Cecile Click, my agent Jim Cypher, my editor Deb Werksman, Rebecca Kilbreath and the entire Sourcebooks team, and several others who wish to remain anonymous.

The Great Sex Secret benefited from the ideas and research in a number of books and articles, all of which are listed in the bibliography. Specific references and quotes are cited in the endnotes, referenced by page numbers and taglines.

Introduction

There are lots of books about sex out there. Why one more? Because there is an important gap in sex research and advice literature: almost no attention has been paid to the ways in which human sexual anatomy makes mutual satisfaction during intercourse a major challenge—or to the work-arounds that some couples have figured out over the years.

Thousands of books, magazines, videos, and websites provide endless ideas about sexual foreplay, positions, and practices, but they tend to avoid the basic structural issues and downplay what would seem to be the ideal finale of sex—orgasms for both partners. There is an implicit assumption that lovers have that part figured out.

But do they? A widely reported indicator of sexual dissatisfaction—as many as 85 percent of women say they don't have orgasms during actual intercourse—has been showing up in research for years. *The Great Sex*

Secret starts with this statistic and addresses some basic questions:

- Why is sexual intercourse so often unfulfilling for women?
- Was there ever a time when this was not true?
- Is it possible for both partners to have orgasms when they make love?
- Are simultaneous orgasms feasible—or desirable?
- What is "great sex," anyway?
- What's technique got to do with it?
- Why do so many lovers have trouble talking about sex?
- What's going on when seemingly happy couples shy away from sex?
- Can sexual passion be kept alive in long-term love relationships?
- Why has sex-advice literature been so unhelpful?

To answer these questions, we'll look at an eclectic array of material from contemporary and historical sources, including the experience of couples who have found their way to mutually satisfying lovemaking. The book presents the following argument:

- Penis-in-vagina sexual intercourse almost always produces an orgasm for men but rarely does for women. This is because the location of the clitoris prevents most women from getting sensitive, appropriate, and sustained stimulation during intercourse. Making love in ways that give both partners full satisfaction is neither easy nor obvious—it doesn't "come naturally."

- Historians tell us that through the ages, the default setting for sexual intercourse has been male satisfaction and female frustration. Several cultures exhorted men to give sexual satisfaction to their partners and even told them that their partners wouldn't get pregnant if they didn't have orgasms—but specific instructions for stimulating the clitoris during intercourse were not provided.

- A persistent myth has been that penetration alone should produce a female orgasm, preferably at the same moment as the man's; simultaneous orgasms have often been touted as the ultimate amorous accomplishment (but without specifics on how to make them happen). Despite today's more sophisticated understanding of human anatomy, this belief persists, and it is one of several reasons that a good number of women fake orgasms during intercourse.

- Lovemaking that is unfulfilling for one partner does not stand the test of time and sows seeds of resentment and unhappiness in a relationship. In recent years, there has been much discussion of "sexless marriages," and the finger is usually pointed at exhaustion in two-career households, male anger about women having more power, and inadequate sexual technique. But figuring out ways for busy couples to be less fatigued, psychoanalyzing the sources of male-female anger, or using better foreplay, exotic positions, and sex toys do not address the real problem.

- Many lovers who start off with a strong sexual connection find that over the years they get bored with sex, don't make love as frequently or for as long as they used to, and aren't "in the mood" at the same moment as their partner. Most sex-advice literature promotes the idea that sexual variety, athleticism, and spontaneity are the ways to keep passion alive in long-term relationships.

- Not true. The key to long-term sexual happiness is having a strong love relationship and finding an effective, mutually satisfactory way to bring both the man and the woman to orgasm while they are together. Three effective approaches have been discovered by couples over the years: first, separate orgasms, with the woman having her climax before or after actual intercourse (first me, then you); second, the woman touching herself during intercourse; and third, the man caressing his partner's clitoris during intercourse. All three approaches reliably bring the woman to orgasm during lovemaking; the second and third can easily produce simultaneous or near-simultaneous orgasms. For full details, see Chapter 6, Three Approaches to Mutual Satisfaction.

- These approaches are almost never discussed in the literature or talked about even among close friends. Laypeople's reticence is regrettable but understandable; the silence of the "experts" is baffling. It appears that almost all researchers and educators are asking the wrong questions and are stuck in an old paradigm of how sexual intercourse is supposed to work. The result is that very few couples get good advice from the literature—or from their parents, their peers, sex education courses, popular culture, and even (or perhaps especially) from erotica and pornography.

- The only way that some lovers have been able to unlock the ancient mystery is by talking honestly and openly with each other about sex. But most people are shy and have had very little practice at putting their sexual likes and dislikes into words. When women have less power within romantic relationships, they are even less likely to speak up in bed. Poor communication is a major obstacle to solving the built-in issues involved in mutually satisfying male-female intercourse.

- Because of this, it's a real challenge for couples to find mutual satisfaction during lovemaking. All too many lovers in each new generation follow the same unsatisfying path as those who came (or did not come) before them. A vast industry of sex material and paraphernalia attempts to alleviate this unhappiness, but very little of it helps.

• Lasting sexual happiness begins when couples confront the mismatches in their sexual anatomies, communicate well, and settle on an approach that reliably gives both partners orgasms when they make love. Making this point and describing the most effective techniques in some detail is what this book is all about.

Chapter One

Disappointment in the Land of Eros: Is There a Design Flaw?

Every day we are bombarded with sex. It comes at us in movies and TV shows, billboards and the Internet, suggestively clad people on the street, and magazine covers in the supermarket check-out counter assaulting us with headlines like "Ten Ways to Drive Him Wild!" The message is not subtle: everyone out there is having great sex, and if you aren't, well, poor you.

Even if we could block out this onslaught of sexual messages, hormones are coursing through our bodies, and most people—especially

> **There is a curious disconnect between our society's hype about "great sex" and recent reports that many couples are unhappy in bed—or not having sex at all.**

adolescents and young adults—are biologically driven to have sexual thoughts with some regularity. John Finley, the late Harvard professor and housemaster, used to joke that the mission of the university was to reduce the amount of time students spend thinking about sex from 85 percent of each day to 55 percent.

Yet for all this ambient sexuality and pressure to join the wonderful sexual party, there are occasional reports from the front lines that things may not be as rosy as we are led to believe:

- In 1985, Ann Landers asked the female readers of her advice column how they felt about making love. She was flooded with more than one hundred thousand letters, with 72 percent of the writers saying they'd much rather be doing something other than having sex. One woman wrote that she found sex with her husband "disgusting and unhygienic," but still loved him and enjoyed their life together.

- More than a decade later, a *New York Times Magazine* article took another poke at the myth of sexual bliss. The article quoted a number of experts, including Dr. Judy Kuriansky, the radio call-in host, who said that by far the most common question she hears is "How do I keep the passion in my marriage alive?" Judith Seifer, a therapist and sex-advice columnist, said that "sexual boredom is the most pandemic dysfunction in this country." And James Petersen, a *Playboy* advice columnist, told of a sign he had spotted on a dirt road in Kentucky: "Choose your rut carefully—you're going to be in it for the next eighteen miles."

- In 2003, an *Atlantic Monthly* article summed up the message of several new books on marriage problems: "A large number of relatively young and otherwise healthy married people are forgoing sex for long periods of time and…many have given it up altogether."

- Then, to top it off, an infamous issue of *Newsweek* featured a cover photo of a couple in bed, the man (wearing an undershirt and bathrobe) peering through half-glasses at his laptop, the woman staring glassy-eyed at the TV while spooning yogurt into her mouth. The banner headline read, "No Sex, Please, We're Married: Are Stress, Kids and Work Killing Romance?" The story inside introduced us to a new acronym: DINS—dual-income, no-sex marriages.

Add to these four reports the fact that half of all new marriages end in divorce (with sexual unhappiness among the leading reasons), and we have the makings of a first-class mystery. How can there be such disconnect between the way sex is *supposed* to be and the day-to-day reality in so many bedrooms? Why are millions of people—

> **The prevailing explanation for sexual unhappiness—that it's caused by dual-career job stress and empowered women—is wrong.**

especially women—so unhappy with sex? How can intercourse, widely touted as the ultimate expression of romantic love, be so disappointing?

The most popular theory is that unhappy or non-existent sex is a by-product of contemporary Western civilization—that the problem stems from two-career households and the stresses of children and modern life. Jane Greer, the online sex therapist for *Redbook*, put it this way:

> Marriage has changed. In the old days the husband was the breadwinner. The wife had the expectation of raising the children and pleasing him. Now they're both working and both taking care of the children, and they're too exhausted and resentful to have sex.

This is a plausible explanation: it *is* challenging for busy couples to carve out the time for sex—and muster the energy—when they come home from a full day's work and have to deal with preparing dinner, bathing children, helping with homework, paying bills, and worrying about the Middle East.

But are stress and exhaustion really the problem? Let's face it; people are rarely too tired to have sex. Anyone with a functioning sexual anatomy, normal hormone levels, and the physical and mental health to respond to another person is a candidate for regular sex, no matter how busy life is. If this is true, something else must be going on in sexually unhappy bedrooms.

Here's another idea: the smoldering anger theory. *Newsweek's* article put it this way: "For many couples, consciously or not, sex has become a weapon. A lot of women out there are mad...men are mad too." What are they mad about? The new family dynamic in which women are no longer second-class citizens and men are expected to make themselves useful around the house in ways that were unthinkable to their fathers. The cartoon character Marge Simpson passed these words of wisdom to her daughter, Lisa: "Marriage is a beautiful thing, but it's also a constant battle for moral superiority."

According to this second hypothesis, festering resentment drives a wedge between spouses—and sex becomes the weapon of choice. The woman withholds sex ("Not tonight; I have a headache...") as a punishment for the man not carrying in the groceries and spending time with the kids, and the man retaliates by ducking his chores and playing even longer poker games with his buddies. In her book, *Against Love: A Polemic*, Laura Kipnis describes "the desire-free zone of long-term marriage":

> Embarrassing, isn't it, how long you can go without it, if you don't remember to have it, and how much more inviting a good night's sleep can seem compared to those over-rehearsed acts.

Caitlin Flanagan, staff writer for the *New Yorker* and *Atlantic Monthly*, puts together the issues of exhausted two-career families and newly-empowered women and paints an even more vivid picture of the sexual fallout:

Pity the poor married man hoping to get a little comfort from the wife at day's end. He must somehow seduce a woman who is economically independent of him, bone tired, philosophically disinclined to have sex unless she is jolly well in the mood, numbingly familiar with his every sexual maneuver, and still doing a slow burn over his failure to wipe down the countertops and fold the dish towels after cooking the kids' dinner. He can hardly be blamed for opting instead to check his email, catch a few minutes of *SportsCenter*, and call it a night.

The stresses of busy couples are real. So is the tectonic shift toward greater equality between men and women. Living in close proximity with another person for a long period of time—even someone you really love—has never been easy, and it's especially difficult nowadays. Flanagan sums up the problem—and suggests a solution:

Marriage remains the most efficient engine of disenchantment yet invented. There is nothing like uninterrupted cohabitation and grinding responsibility to cast a clear, unforgiving light on the object of desire...The element that regularly restores a marriage to something with an aspect of romance...is sex.

Flanagan is suggesting that the way to escape this miasma of exhaustion and resentment is to *just do it*. This sounds logical. Couples need to leapfrog over their daily cares and woes and have terrific sex! Then they'll feel better—and get along better the rest of the time.

But it can't be that simple. If jumping into the sack were all it took to overcome modern couple problems, people would have figured it out long ago. There's got to be more to it than that.

Back to job stress and women being less dependent on their husbands. If these are truly the sources of the problem, then it would be logical that marital sex was better when women were full-time housewives and didn't have to fret about a job outside the home. In the 1950s, middle-class women had less demanding lives and were less of a threat to the male ego. They had plenty of time to take care of all the household work during the day and focus on being sexually pleasing at night. But the evidence suggests that women were only pseudo-happy in the fifties; Betty Friedan's trailblazing book, *The Feminine Mystique*, said that in this era, many women actually felt like "a passive, empty mirror." And what's more, the sex was lousy. Surveys and personal testimonials tell us that most women in this era found sex one-sided and unsatisfying, but were hesitant to speak up because they were economically and psychologically dependent on their husbands.

Speak up about what? About the fact that sex with their husbands was almost always a frustrating experience—to put it bluntly, that they were not having orgasms during intercourse.

Nowadays, women are more empowered and independent. So have they spoken up and addressed this problem? Apparently a lot of them haven't. A consistent finding of sex research is that between 65 and 85 percent of women do not regularly have an orgasm during sexual intercourse.

> The real reason for sexual unhappiness is dissatisfaction with sex itself. Men's and women's sexual anatomies just don't fit together in a way that readily satisfies both partners.

The evidence suggests a radically different theory about the sexual malaise of so many couples today. Is it possible that the trouble stems from unhappiness *with sex itself*? Is it conceivable that this dissatisfaction has existed for centuries and is surfacing now (albeit indirectly) because women have more power and are less dependent on men? Could it be that what's really driving the anger and resentment of many women is deep disappointment that, after a sexy beginning, their love life has become an "eighteen-mile rut" of frustration? Have we been looking in the wrong place for answers to contemporary sexual unhappiness? Could the root causes of all the complaints be a set of deep, built-in male-female incompatibilities—the ways in which their sexual anatomies don't fit together—that make mutually satisfying lovemaking a challenge even under the best of circumstances?

These are important, troubling questions—and it's amazing how rarely they are talked about. Even with sex, sex, sex all around us, there is very little honest discourse about what really goes on in bed—and about the ways in which men and women connect and don't connect when they make love. For a sexually liberated nation, we are remarkably reserved about the most intimate details of sexual intercourse. How can this be?

Well, people are shy. Most of us are embarrassed to ask even our closest friends about what really happens when they make love. The average adult has had fairly limited sexual experience (between one and ten lifetime partners), and is naturally curious about what other couples do: Have they discovered something better? Do they have secrets they're not sharing? But people very rarely ask such questions.

Furthermore, in conversations about sex, there is a built-in filter that keeps both good and bad news from being talked about very much. If people find sex disappointing, they are loath to admit it; if sex is amazing, people don't want to seem boastful (only jerks brag about sex). So most day-to-day chatter about sex is pretty superficial, using humor to disguise discomfort and shedding very little light on what lovemaking is *really* like.

If couples turn to sex advice books and videos (which are easier and easier to buy), do they get better answers? With a few exceptions, the literature is quite unhelpful on the core issues, filling its pages and video footage with ever more exotic sexual positions, practices, and devices. And highly explicit erotica and pornographic materials propagate the myth of constant sexual ecstasy, endless lovemaking, and effortless female orgasms. Even if we find all this titillating, we know in our hearts that it's not reality.

What about parents' talks with their pubescent children? Basic anatomy may be described, awkwardly. HIV and AIDS are often warned about, apocalyptically. Condoms may be recommended, squeamishly. But parents find it really difficult to talk to their kids about intercourse and sexual pleasure, much less the challenges involved in making love with mutual satisfaction. Maybe they don't know where to begin. Maybe they are nervous about opening themselves up to questions about their *own* sex lives, past and present. And maybe they fear that such discussions will bring them face to face with the fact that their sons and daughters are growing into sexual beings. Kids are also quite adept at avoiding explicit sex talks—especially if it means thinking about their parents in sexual terms. Mom and Dad, like, "doing it?" No way!

How about sex education programs in schools? Almost without exception, they have failed to deal forthrightly with sexual intercourse—just the plumbing, ma'am, along with assurances that sex is a mystical thing between a man and a woman that's really wonderful—but sorry, we can't go into the details.

What all this adds up to is a societal failure to confront the most important "facts of life." Almost all of us grow up without ever hearing a frank discussion of what's involved in having mutually gratifying sex. Caught between the myth that good sex just "comes naturally" and the emerging media consensus that sexless marriage is the norm, couples can be forgiven for feeling pretty confused.

And yet there's a strong romantic current in our society, a stubborn belief that sex and love should go hand in hand, that primal sexual urges can somehow be yoked to love and that their union is true happiness. Bringing these two strands together is every couple's dream—but that means working out some very real male-female sexual differences.

Are Men and Women Sexually Mismatched?

To understand these differences, we need to go back to the basics of human sexual anatomy and look at the way lovers have mated through the millennia. At the level of simple reproduction, our sexual anatomies are well matched. The aroused woman's lubricated vagina is perfectly designed to welcome the aroused man's erect penis. A man's brain is hardwired to find the vagina's embrace highly pleasurable, and during intercourse these circuits fire and most men have an orgasm after just a few minutes of intercourse. Millions of sperm are ejaculated, and if there's nothing blocking their way and it's the right time of the month, one of them has a good chance of reaching and fertilizing an egg. This design has worked very efficiently over the millennia—the planet now has six billion living souls.

But when it comes to sexual pleasure, men's and women's bodies are not such a perfect match. What is most exciting for a man—his penis thrusting inside his partner's vagina—is often pleasurable for a woman (especially initial penetration, since the outer third of the vagina is most sensitive) but rarely produces an orgasm. That's because the clitoris—the woman's primary orgasm-producing spot—is located a little distance from the entrance to the vagina. During penis-in-vagina sex, the clitoris is not directly stimulated, which is why most women report that they do not have a climax during actual intercourse. Alfred Kinsey, the American sex researcher, once said that believing that female orgasms can be produced through penetration alone is like believing that the earth is flat.

A second male-female difference is that women need a different kind of stimulation than men to reach an orgasm—more sustained, more sensitive, and more tuned to the unique design of the clitoris (which is the only part of the human body designed solely for sexual

> **Two factors—the location of the clitoris and the type of stimulation a woman requires to reach orgasm—result in very few women reaching orgasm during intercourse.**

pleasure, with six thousand to eight thousand sensory nerve endings, far more than the tongue or the fingertips or a man's penis). Natalie Angier captures some of the nuances of the clitoris and how closely it is linked to the emotions in her book, *Woman: An Intimate Geography*:

> If you are frightened, it becomes numb. If you are uninterested or disgusted, it remains mute. If you are thrilled and strong, it is a taut little baton, leading the way, cajoling here, quickening there, andante, allegro, crescendo, refrain.

The type of stimulation that produces an orgasm for most women is different than it is for a man. For example, a stream of water or a vibrator do almost nothing for a man's penis but can be highly arousing on a woman's clitoris. Another difference: if clitoral stimulation is interrupted, or if it's too rough or intense, the woman can lose her place and need to start over.

What is the result of these two male-female differences? During conventional intercourse, a woman doesn't get the kind of sensitive, well-tuned, and continuous stimulation necessary to bring her to orgasm. Straightforward, unassisted, penis-in-vagina intercourse is almost always sexually rewarding for a man—and rarely is for a woman.

This is an important insight—yet there seems to be a conspiracy of silence about these male-female sexual asymmetries. They are almost never described in sex education classes, parental talks, peer banter, and other sex materials. As a result, most people are in the dark until their first sexual encounters—and unfortunately that's not a time when couples talk openly and honestly if things aren't going the way they're supposed to go.

> For some reason, sex literature and the popular media almost never discuss the built-in reasons why most women don't have orgasms during intercourse.

In fact, when men and women have intercourse for the first time, they tend to react somewhat differently. It's natural for them to compare two-person sex with their own experience with solo sex (virtually all males and most females masturbate). For the man, intercourse is usually a major improvement because of the way the lubricated vagina stimulates his penis. For the woman, early experiences with intercourse are often a disappointment because her clitoris gets little or no stimulation. Here's how a seventeen-year-old described her first experience:

> The first time I had intercourse I was lying there thinking, *You mean this is IT? Am I supposed to be thrilled by this?* It wasn't that it hurt me or anything, because it didn't. It just didn't feel like anything to me. I figured there must be something wrong with me, so I didn't say a word to him.

Add to this confused disappointment a woman's fear of getting pregnant, her worries about sexual infections, and her uncertainty about the emotional side of things (Does he really love me? Will he dump me after we do this? Will he tell his friends?), and it's no wonder that many women secretly conclude that intercourse is vastly overrated.

A generation ago, when most couples didn't rush into intercourse, they spent more time on first base (kissing), second base (touching above the waist), and third base (touching each others' genitals). This kind of extended "outercourse" without penetration can be satisfying for a woman because the man is more likely to bring her to orgasm. But nowadays, a lot of couples charge around third base and head straight for home, sometimes on the first date, while others "hook up," engaging in quickie oral sex with most of the focus on male pleasure. (Which "base" is fellatio? Third in terms of getting pregnant, home in terms of sexual infections.)

Couples who progress rapidly to vaginal or oral penetration tend to learn less about each other's bodies, and men who begin with this kind of sex may never get acquainted with the all-important "geography" of lovemaking—what gives a woman deep satisfaction. Here's how a woman described this kind of unsatisfying early lovemaking:

> We rush into it—or let our partners rush us into it. We end up fucking with great intensity, swept off our feet just like in the movies, and swept under the rug when it comes to climaxes.

A Design Flaw?

Why do these sexual asymmetries between men and women exist? What possible purpose is served by the woman's orgasm-producing nerve endings being in a place where the movement of a man's penis in the

vagina does not give her maximum pleasure? Why isn't
the body laid out so that a woman's orgasm can occur
during the procreative act? Everything in the body is
supposed to have a purpose, so is the placement of the
clitoris a design error?

Let's take the argument a step further. Is the female
orgasm even necessary to our species' survival, since a
woman does not need one to get pregnant?

Not so fast. Sexual satisfaction is just as important
for women, both mentally and physically. In fact, a
woman's orgasm is more glorious than a man's in meas-
urable ways. When a man reaches orgasm, he has three
or four major contractions followed by a few irregular
minor ones, all confined to his genital area. When a
woman climaxes, she has five to eight major contractions, then nine to fifteen minor ones, all of them felt
throughout her pelvic area.

Clearly, female orgasms are *fun*. But do they serve an
evolutionary purpose? Over the years, various theories
have been advanced, including:

- That a woman is slightly more likely to get pregnant when she has an orgasm because the cervix
  pulls more sperm into the uterus during a climax.
- That when a woman has an orgasm during intercourse, oxytocin, the "bonding hormone," is
  released, and she has affectionate feelings and a
  desire to be close to her partner, which confers a

Darwinian advantage by helping the couple stay together through the vicissitudes of life.

• That a woman's health is improved when she has orgasms as part of lovemaking because pelvic engorgement is reduced, she gets more of a cardio-vascular workout, estrogen levels are boosted, endorphins are released (which reduce stress and pain), and her immune system and general well-being are enhanced.

But for these theories to be valid, female orgasms would have to have been a regular feature of intercourse through the millennia, with women who had during-intercourse orgasms surviving and women who didn't have them dying out. There's strong evidence that female orgasms during intercourse have *not* been the norm throughout history. This casts serious doubt on the theory that female orgasms exist because they conferred any kind of selective advantage.

In her book, *The Case of the Female Orgasm: Bias in the Science of Evolution*, biology professor Elisabeth Lloyd trashes the adaptationist theories, arguing that they work backwards from the assumption that the female orgasm *must* have an evolutionary function and ignore lots of evidence to the contrary. Lloyd presents an alternative theory: that the *potential* for female orgasm is a by-product of embryological development in all mammals. In humans, the same fetal tissues develop into a penis or a clitoris starting in the eighth week of pregnancy, depending on whether they get a dose of male or female hormones. Both sexual organs have the same origins and, years later, both can produce orgasms. But because of the location of the clitoris, females' potential for orgasm is realized only under certain conditions—which rarely include basic intercourse. When women do have orgasms with their partners, some of the advantages kick in, including bonding and health benefits. But Lloyd disposes of the notion that these have been evolutionarily purposeful.

So why have our anatomies evolved in this apparently incompatible way? Why is it so difficult for women to get deep sexual pleasure during intercourse? How can millions of sexually frustrated women be part of nature's design?

We can explore this evolutionary puzzle by dividing sexually active heterosexual women into those who don't have an orgasm during intercourse (65 to 85 percent of women are in this category, according to most research) and those who do (the remaining 15 to 35 percent). Among the former, there are three common

> **Lovemaking that is one-sided and unfulfilling for one partner does not stand the test of time and can sow seeds of resentment and unhappiness in a relationship.**

scenarios: Wham, Bam, Thank You, Ma'am (the man has an orgasm and does little or nothing to give pleasure to his partner); the man tries to give his partner an orgasm but fails; and the woman fakes an orgasm. In each case, lovemaking ends without the woman getting deep sexual satisfaction. The next three chapters explore each of these scenarios in turn.

Chapter Two

Wham, Bam, Thank You, Ma'am: The Long History of One-Sided Sex

In the first no-female-orgasm scenario, Wham, Bam, Thank You, Ma'am, the man engages in a little foreplay, stimulates the clitoris just enough to produce some lubrication, enters the vagina, pumps to orgasm, rolls over, and goes to sleep. This approach has also been called 3-2-1 sex: three minutes of foreplay, two minutes of intercourse, and one orgasm—his. A man who "makes love" this way gets satisfaction himself but gives little or none in return.

Why would a man act so selfishly in bed? In some cases, it's because he's ignorant of how a woman's body works: he assumes that what feels good for him must also feel good for her. Or perhaps he's lazy about putting in the time and effort needed to give equal satisfaction to his partner. Or it could be that he's selfish and doesn't give a damn. Men in the last category would probably enjoy this joke:

Question: How can you tell if a woman has had an orgasm?

Answer: Who *cares*?

Or maybe Wham-Bam men are uncomfortable with the intense emotions surrounding a woman's orgasm and the deeper relationship (and, God forbid, *commitment*) that it might portend.

Whatever the thought process, the result is the same: a sexually unsatisfied woman.

Over the years, lots of women have experienced this kind of sex, and they may have felt they had little choice but to put up with it. In another time and place, women were advised to "lie back and think of England." Nowadays women with partners like these are more likely to multitask, tolerating their partners during intercourse while mentally planning tomorrow's dinner.

Two contemporary jokes show that this problem is very much on people's minds:

- Lawyer to witness in court: "Are you sexually active?" Woman: "No, I just lie there."
- What do women do after sex?

  5 percent fall asleep

  5 percent take a shower

  5 percent read a romance novel

  85 percent go get their vibrators

We smile, but the humor has an edge to it. Over time, the emotional costs of one-sided sex are high. Here is one woman's poignant testimony:

Sex was something that was "done to me." I felt an incredible lack of mutuality and lack of control. I became, over time, a passive instrument for my husband's pleasure. I felt very distanced from him during intercourse. I had the sense that he was relating to his own fantasies while he was having contact with me. He later told me this was often the case. It was not just my husband's fault...Neither of us had people close enough to talk to about the problem, nor a sense of other people going through similar things. I felt sexually destroyed.

Another woman shared this angry fantasy:

We are having intercourse. I have an orgasm before him. I pull off of his penis and lie beside him, enjoying myself fully. He's very hurt. I say: "I should, but I don't want to continue." (His words to me on former occasions.) He insists. I scream at him: "Selfish pig! Can't you take what you dish out? Now you know what it feels like most of the time for a woman having sex." You're supposed to say: "It's okay. Just lie back and enjoy yourself. I'll wait until next time."

How many couples are in the Wham-Bam mode? We don't have accurate statistics on couples today (a result of the right questions not being asked and the fact that a lot of women are probably fibbing), but there is growing evidence that throughout human history, this is the way the vast majority of human beings have experienced sexual intercourse. In her comprehensive book, *Sex in History*, Reay Tannahill says that for thousands of years, sex was an overwhelmingly male-dominated, one-sided affair. In his book, *Human Sexuality in Four Perspectives*, William Davenport concurs: "In most of the societies for which we have data, it is reported that men take the initiative and, without extended foreplay, proceed vigorously toward climax without much regard for achieving synchrony with the woman's orgasm."

Perhaps it's naive to think it would be otherwise. In most societies, men have regarded women as chattel—useful for preparing meals, doing domestic chores, providing them with sexual pleasure, and bearing and raising children. Marriages with mutual sexual satisfaction seem to have been a rarity, and a woman's "right" to an orgasm was unheard of until very recently. No doubt there were always couples who found their way to mutual satisfaction in bed, but they seem to have been few and far between—and they seem to have kept very quiet about the techniques they used.

> **Historians tell us that for thousands of years, the default setting for sexual intercourse has been male satisfaction and female frustration.**

Cluelessness and insensitivity about female sexual satisfaction were especially prevalent among Victorian-era Brits and Americans—with the addition of a stultifying layer of prudery and refusal to see women (or at least "good" women) as sexual beings. In the middle of the nineteenth century, the British surgeon William Acton proclaimed, "I should say that the majority of women (happily for society) are not very much troubled with sexual feelings of any kind. Love of home, of children, and of domestic duties are the only passions they feel."

In their scholarly book *Intimate Matters: A History of Sexuality in America*, John D'Emilio and Estelle Freedman describe the ignorance of nineteenth-century Americans about female sexuality and the social mores that forbade "proper" women from showing sexual pleasure, even (or perhaps especially) within marriage. The book says that few women in this era had orgasms during intercourse, and many regarded sex as a family duty with little appeal. One woman wrote to a friend: "It does nothing for me except disgust me…He calls it pleasure, but I'd rather be with friends or on a picnic or something."

Tannahill has this poignant observation on the plight of women—and men—in this era:

It was not altogether surprising that the gentle and submissive Victorian wife should have been thought of as undersexed. Her repressed upbringing, the refinement and "spirituality" that were forced upon her, and her ignorance of physiology all helped to make her so, and even a woman who was not physically revolted by intercourse needed very delicate handling if she were to enjoy the experience. It was a task for which few Victorian husbands were equipped. They had their own problems, their own inhibitions, and making love to "the angel of the house" in the awareness that she was concealing a gently-bred disgust was scarcely conducive to a satisfactory performance.

Did any of the Victorians find a way out of the problem? One reflective gentleman quoted in *Intimate Matters* wrote to a friend: "I have a sense of guilt when I have relations with her and she does not enjoy them as much as I do. The fact that she's not getting an orgasm takes the pleasure of intercourse away from me." But this well-intentioned lover didn't seem to know what to do, and most men either accepted the male-female pleasure gap as a fact of life or concluded that their mates were undersexed, frigid, or dysfunctional. Needless to say, prostitution and extramarital affairs with more sexually expressive women thrived in an environment in which spousal sex so often lacked mutual passion.

There was one curious exception to the nineteenth-century mindset. The leaders of a small utopian community in Oneida, New York, required that men practice *coitus reservatus* as a form of communal birth control. Couples were taught to engage in extensive foreplay, and men were instructed on how to give their partners climaxes during intercourse (using a carefully specified position with the man entering the vagina from behind) while holding back their own orgasms.

But this was a fleeting aberration. Until well into the twentieth century, it appears that the vast majority of women were sexually frustrated after intercourse. Most spent their lives in an orgasm deficit, but they lacked the vocabulary and the conceptual framework to put their finger on the problem.

The obvious sexual outlet—masturbation—was taboo. In fact, beginning around 1700, a private act that had been regarded with benign indifference for millennia was virtually criminalized in the Western world. Boys and girls were told that masturbation was morally wrong and physically harmful—and the Catholic Church ranked masturbation as a mortal sin, right up there with rape and murder. The title of a pamphlet published in 1710 captures the spirit: *Onania, or the Heinous Sin of Self-Pollution, and All Its Frightful Consequences, in both Sexes, Consider'd with Spiritual and Physical Advice to those, who have already injur'd themselves by this abominable practice.* The French clinician Simon Tissot claimed that masturbation depleted vital bodily fluids and led to feebleness and vice. In the mid-nineteenth century, masturbation was even thought to cause tuberculosis.

In his book, *Making Sex: Body and Gender from the Greeks to Freud*, Thomas Laqueur describes the Victorian propaganda about "the suicidal masturbator whose faculties are greatly impaired, whose thinking is impractical, memory weak, and body reduced to skin and bones… [who] will never find comfort in married love and thus contributes to the social monstrosity of sterility."

In the United States, John Harvey Kellogg went on a campaign against masturbation and wrote *Plain Facts for Old and Young*, listing thirty-nine warning signs (including moodiness, sleeplessness, lassitude, nail-biting, pimples, use of tobacco, bad appetite, and general grumpiness). Kellogg believed that a bland diet could control the ravages of sexual passion, and he developed and successfully marketed Corn Flakes to help solve the problem. But he didn't think that eating his cereal was sufficient to stop masturbation; he also recommended childhood circumcision (without anesthesia), silver sutures across the foreskin, and carbolic acid applied to the clitoris.

Attitudes on masturbation gradually mellowed in the twentieth century, but it wasn't until 1972 that the American Medical Association finally declared that masturbation was a normal sexual act.

Sexually frustrated women who believed all this nonsense and refrained from masturbation (abstainers were probably more numerous among girls and women than among

> **Until well into the twentieth century, it appears that the vast majority of women were sexually frustrated after intercourse.**

boys and men) had no sexual outlet, and their libidinous urges built up like steam in a pressure cooker. Something had to give, and a number of women exhibited a variety of physical and psychological ailments that Freud and others called "hysteria." The original meaning of this word is "womb disease," and it was first diagnosed in Egypt four thousand years ago.

Here is a composite of the symptoms of hysteria as described by doctors over the years: fainting, edema, nervousness, insomnia, sensations of heaviness in the abdomen, muscle spasms, shortness of breath, loss of appetite for food or for sex with the approved male partner, and sometimes a tendency to cause trouble for others, particularly members of the patient's immediate family. Doctors came to believe that hysteria was caused by insufficient sexual intercourse, not enough sexual gratification, or both. Not a bad diagnosis! But rather than addressing the *source* of this sexual frustration, doctors persisted in treating women with these symptoms as if they were suffering from an illness.

The descriptions of hysteria listed above come from a remarkable book by Rachel Maines, *The Technology of Orgasm*. The book goes on to document that in the late nineteenth and early twentieth centuries, many middle-class American women went to their doctors to be treated for these ailments. What did the doctors do? They applied vulvular massage—in plain English, they stimulated their patients' clitorises with their fingers and brought them to orgasm. This was a highly lucrative business for a number of years: patients didn't die of the "illness," but they didn't recover either; the treatment was inexpensive to administer, and patients kept coming back for more. It was a cash cow.

Maines also describes how a good number of nineteenth-century British and American women with symptoms of hysteria went to medically supervised spas for "hydrotherapy." A variety of ingenious machines directed jets of water at women's vulvas, bringing

Not long after the invention of electricity, the electro-mechanical vibrator was introduced in the 1880s, and doctors were quick to see its potential to ease hysteria in women.

on the orgasms they were not getting during sexual intercourse. Women who visited these spas felt a whole lot better and became regular customers—and the doctors and proprietors reaped huge profits.

All this is hard to believe. But Maines's book has scholarly evidence that it really did happen, not just in the 1800s and early 1900s, but, in the case of genital massage by physicians, all the way back to the first century AD. We can only shake our heads in wonder. Doctors were doing a job that nobody else would do—not husbands, not lovers, not the frustrated women themselves.

Surely, these doctors knew that what they were doing was sexual. Not so, says Maines. In the Victorian era, there was a strong belief in some quarters that the vagina was the only truly sexual part of girls' and of women's bodies and that female orgasms were caused only by penetration. (Because of this belief, a huge fuss was made when the speculum and the tampon were first introduced; wild stories circulated about females reacting with sexual delight when either object was inserted into the vagina.) A willful ignorance about the clitoris in some parts of the medical profession (it wasn't even mentioned in many medical diagrams or textbooks of this era) seems to have allowed doctors to believe that stimulating a woman's external genitalia was a *medical* and not a sexual act. The fact that doctors did not identify their patients' reactions to massage as orgasmic says a lot about their own sex lives: if they did not recognize a female orgasm when it happened in their examining room, they must never have experienced one in their bedrooms.

Maines contends that doctors, far from getting prurient delight from these "treatments," found them tedious and exhausting. Because clitoral stimulation requires some skill and the level of dexterity among doctors varied widely, some sessions took as long as an hour. Long-suffering medics delegated the job to midwives or assistants whenever possible.

Then American technological ingenuity came to the rescue. Not long after the invention of electricity, the electromechanical vibrator was introduced in the 1880s, and doctors were quick to see its potential. Using a vibrator, a doctor could bring a woman to orgasm in only five to ten minutes, eliminating the fatigue factor and making it possible to see more patients every day. For a period of about thirty years, vibrators were a staple in many doctors' offices, and countless women received regular treatments.

But just after the turn of the twentieth century, two developments put a stop to this lucrative business. First, several American companies started producing low-cost vibrators for home use and advertised them in mainstream women's magazines. (It was in these magazines that Rachel Maines first stumbled upon this phenomenon, leading her to uncover the rest of the story.) Spotting these ads, lots of women must have said to themselves, "Why pay for visits to my doctor when I can administer the same treatment in the privacy of my own home?"

Second, around 1920, a number of stag movies were released that featured the vibrator in raunchy sex scenes. The stag movies stripped away the social camouflage and revealed that what all those doctors were doing to their patients (and what some women were doing at home) was *sexual.* Doctors stopped using vibrators to treat women for hysteria and didn't go back to the more laborious procedure they had used before, because obviously that was sexual, too. Women who were using vibrators realized that they had purchased a sex toy and were (gasp!) *masturbating.* Women brought up to believe that masturbation was harmful and wrong threw away their machines with considerable embarrassment, and advertisements for vibrators disappeared from women's magazines.

At this point in the early 1920s, when the medical "treatment" of orgasm-deprived women was brought to a halt, Americans had arrived at a sexual crossroads. Would the sorry state of Wham, Bam, Thank You, Ma'am lovemaking change? Would people find ways to improve lovemaking techniques now that they knew more about the role of the clitoris and the importance of regular orgasms to women's health and happiness? Would men stop defining women's sexual unhappiness as an illness? And would women speak up more force-fully for equal satisfaction in the bedroom?

No, no, no, and no. The evidence is that few people integrated the new insights into their sex lives and few women were willing and able to be more assertive about their sexual needs. Continued problems with open and honest communication about sex—and the stubborn-ness of the old paradigms in people's heads—prevented this from happening. How long did this state of affairs continue? Here are three pieces of evidence that give us some indication:

• In 1935, a feisty Viennese woman wrote to Sig-mund Freud complaining about men's unsatisfac-tory lovemaking techniques. Freud's response was very telling; he blamed the asymmetrical designs of human sexual anatomy and threw up his hands about what men (or women) might do to rectify the situation:

Dear Madam,
I think that you are right that most men are egotistical and ignorant in their sexual life and don't care enough for the sexual satisfaction of the female. The main fault, however, is yet not on the side of man. Much more of it seems there is a neglect on the side of nature, which is interested only that the purpose of the sexual act is

being attained while it shows indifference as to whether the woman gets full satisfaction or not. The reasons for this strange neglect, about which the female rightfully complains, are not yet recognized with certainty.
Yours very truly,
Freud

- In 1992, Richard Rhodes wrote in his extraordinarily candid sexual autobiography, *Making Love, An Erotic Odyssey*:

It's appalling that men, willing to invest thought and energy in learning a sport...won't invest thought and energy in learning how to play generously at sex. On the evidence, far too many men are sexually selfish and self-centered, reverting in the intimacy of the bedroom to mommy's darlings, taking rather than giving, not required, as girls are required from earliest childhood, to pay attention to needs other than their own. Women complain, but bedroom chauvinism is so all-pervasive they hardly know where to turn.

- In 2002, Kim Cattrall, the actress who played the sexually liberated Samantha Jones in the TV series *Sex and the City*, wrote a sex advice book in which she confessed that she was sexually unsatisfied for most of her adult life:

Many men don't know how to enable a woman to reach orgasm, and many women are not informed or confident enough to tell men what they need to do. I've discovered that the whole subject is essentially taboo. No one wants to admit it that millions of women have unsatisfying sex lives and that most men do not know what to do about it.

> **Women who find themselves in relationships where they are subservient to men often feel they have no choice but to accept unsatisfying lovemaking.**

Could it be that, despite all the gains of the last century, one-sided sex is still the norm in many bedrooms? Yes, because four perennial factors are still very much in play:

- The asymmetries between men's and women's bodies
- Men's ignorance about giving women sexual satisfaction
- The chronic disempowerment of women, leading them to refrain from speaking up
- The lack of honest communication in bed

These factors seem to be keeping a good portion of each new generation of lovers in the same one-sided pattern of making love. We might almost call Wham-Bam—that formula for female frustration—the default setting for sexual intercourse.

But can't this deeply ingrained pattern be changed? Isn't it possible for women to speak up for their own sexual needs? Can't men listen to their partners and *get it*? There certainly have been attempts to improve upon Wham-Bam sex. The next chapter looks at some of them.

Chapter Three

No Female Orgasm— But He Tried

Over the millennia, several cultures have made earnest efforts to give women their fair share of sexual satisfaction.

- In the Jewish *Halakhah*, a body of tradition and law that goes back thousands of years, husbands are told that it is their *responsibility* to sexually satisfy their wives. It is considered a *mitzvah* (a commandment and a good deed) for a man to share sexual pleasure with his wife, especially on the Sabbath. This ancient teaching is definitely on the right track! The problem is that the admonition was not accompanied by *details*, without which most couples are still in the dark. There's no evidence that Jewish women have done any better than women in other cultures at getting real sexual satisfaction during intercourse.

- The ancient Chinese Tao sex manuals said that a man must, without fail, bring his partner to orgasm. The clitoris (dubbed the Jewel Terrace) was correctly identified as the center of female sexual pleasure, and a woman's orgasm was said to be as important to the man as it was to the woman.

But neither the Chinese documents—nor the sex manuals of ancient India—contained details on exactly how the woman was to be brought to orgasm. The *Kama Sutra* and the Tao and Tantric books do not

> **In some cultures men have made serious efforts to give equal sexual satisfaction to women—but have lacked the all-important details on how to make it happen.**

have a single picture of a clitoris being touched by either partner during intercourse, and they don't contain instructions on how to work around the asymmetries of males' and females' bodies.

So despite the rhetoric about mutual pleasure, the how-to of female orgasm was left to the imagination. The sexologists of ancient Asia did no better than those of other cultures at figuring out the geography of making love. The bottom line in these books is one of men pursuing their appetite for a variety of sexual positions and having lots of high-quality orgasms—their own.

• In Tudor and Stuart England and early Colonial America, the function of the clitoris was also widely understood. And in the nineteenth century, some religious leaders had a remarkably enlightened view of the role of female pleasure. In 1848, the Bishop of Philadelphia, Francis Patrick Kenrick, recommended orgasms for women and strongly advised men to give their wives sexual pleasure. Great concept—but again, no details.

Did these Jewish, Chinese, and English advocates of female pleasure hold back secrets that they didn't pass along to the masses? Is it possible that they whispered their valuable insights to a highly satisfied elite and never wrote them down? This seems improbable, given the graphic nature of the illustrations and text in surviving manuals and the highly explicit stone carvings in parts of Asia. It's more likely that through the ages, sexual-advice givers had simply not figured out a straightforward, practical route to mutual sexual satisfaction during intercourse.

Another question: is it possible that women in this era knew what it would take to have equal satisfaction in bed, but were too disempowered to share their insights? Laqueur wonders whether "those who knew—women— did not write and those who wrote—men—did not know." Perhaps. But when women did write about sex during the Renaissance, Laqueur found that they followed the male party line. It appears that among many men and women, the role of the clitoris and the glories of female pleasure were well understood, but ways to reliably bring a woman to orgasm during intercourse were not.

The bottom line: over the years, eager readers of even the most sophisticated sex manuals were getting *exhortations, not explanations.*

And why were men (at least in some cultures) being exhorted so insistently to give their partners an orgasm? Perhaps it was out of genuine concern for female pleasure, but there may also have been another, more existential motive. For more than a thousand years, it was believed that a woman would not get pregnant if she did not have an orgasm. This misconception seems to have originated with Hippocrates around 600 BC and was perpetuated (or recreated) by a succession of "experts" through the years, including the Greek physician Galen in the second century AD and the Arabic writer Rhazes in the tenth century. The idea stemmed from the belief that women's sexual functions mirrored those of men. If a man's orgasm accompanies the ejaculation of semen, then a woman's orgasm must be similarly tied to procreation. No orgasm, no baby.

Based on this theory, it was widely believed that prostitutes did not get pregnant because they did not have orgasms with their clients. And if a woman became pregnant after being raped, it was assumed she must have had an orgasm and was therefore guilty of licentiousness and adultery and needed to be put to death.

Taking this logic a step further, some early scientists asserted that for conception to take place, a man and woman needed to have *simultaneous* orgasms. The theory was that if a woman had an orgasm *before* her

> **Through the years, there's been a persistent myth that male penetration produces a female orgasm—but the evidence is that this almost never happens.**

partner, her cervix would clamp shut and no sperm would be able to get into the uterus. If she had her orgasm *after* the man, her egg would still be in the ovary and when the sperm entered the uterus, they would all die before conception could take place. Perfect synchronization of orgasms was therefore essential to procreation.

Wouldn't men, believing that they could never sire a child if their wives didn't have orgasms during intercourse, be highly motivated to figure out the mechanics of mutual satisfaction? It stands to reason—and yet men seem to have gone only part of the way down this road. Many understood how important it was to stimulate the clitoris, but then caressed it only enough to get the woman aroused and lubricated—as part of the warm-up act—and rarely sustained the stimulation long enough to bring the woman all the way to orgasm.

Why didn't men finish what they started? Perhaps they found the mechanics of clitoral stimulation during intercourse inappropriate or awkward. Perhaps lovers didn't know what a female orgasm felt and sounded like, and assumed they had done their job if the woman lubricated and expressed *some* pleasure. Perhaps their partners had never experienced an orgasm and couldn't identify its absence during lovemaking. Perhaps, in the heat of passion, men reverted to sexual selfishness, casting aside their attempts to bring their partners to orgasm in the headlong rush toward their own enjoyment. Or perhaps women knew all along that having an orgasm had nothing to do with getting pregnant and faked pleasure to keep their men in the game and conceive the children they longed to hold.

It's amazing. Even with the future of the species supposedly hanging in the balance, most women *still* didn't get real sexual satisfaction when they had intercourse.

Over time, the belief that conception couldn't happen without a female orgasm was undermined by repeated cases of women getting pregnant without sexual enjoyment (including by rape)—and women failing to get pregnant despite rapturous lovemaking. As the belief that the survival of humanity did *not* depend on female orgasms eroded (this occurred around 1700, according to Laqueur), it was logical for men to conclude that they were off the hook when it came to fully satisfying their partners.

So did men stop trying? Not all of them. Presumably

many good-hearted, well-intentioned men continued to try to satisfy their partners in bed. What motivated them? It could have been a woman getting up the courage to tell him, directly or indirectly, that she was not happy with their lovemaking. It could have been a man's genuine concern for his partner's pleasure and happiness. It's possible that the man discovered that having an orgasm with a partner who is just *lying there* was not as exciting as it was when she was reveling in genuine sexual pleasure. Maybe it dawned on men that one-sided sex, while satisfying in the short run, lacked an important dimension of mutuality and joy. And perhaps men realized that an unsatisfied partner wasn't conducive to a happy relationship—in other words, that Wham-Bam sex was not in their long-term best interests.

Some or all of these motivations have always prodded men in the direction of being less selfish in bed. But four changes in the twentieth century did even more to improve the chances of mutually satisfying intercourse:

- Attitudes about sex became more liberated.
- Expressions of sexual pleasure, even among "good" women, were increasingly accepted.
- Many women gained a measure of power and independence.
- Reliable birth control eliminated one of the biggest worries—getting pregnant.

With these revolutionary developments came the *potential* for women to be more assertive and articulate about their sexual desires and the *possibility* that couples might come to see intercourse as an arena for mutual enjoyment and fun—not just procreation and male pleasure. Given the long history of Wham-Bam sex, this was potentially a profound shift—especially the idea that intercourse could *and should* give sexual satisfaction and emotional fulfillment to a woman.

But *wanting* to make this happen has never been enough. Making love in a way that is mutually satisfying has never been easy or obvious. To overcome the built-in barriers, a couple has to be able to *talk* about what's working and what isn't and experiment with solutions, giving each other honest feedback at every turn. While some creative lovers have found their way to mutual satisfaction, they are the exception, and the reason is most people's very low comfort level talking about sex—all stemming from the continuing shame and ambivalence that hovers around the subject in most homes and sex-education classes.

Many women—even some feminists who are highly liberated in other spheres of life—are not comfortable enough with their own sexuality to point out what their partners should do. They're reluctant to demand equal time in the orgasm department—and perhaps most important, don't have a clear sense of how mutual pleasure can occur during intercourse.

Women who don't communicate their sexual needs are going to have to put up with clueless, unsatisfying lovemaking year after year. After all, a man isn't born knowing how to give pleasure to a woman any more than a woman is born knowing how to cook. And where are men supposed to learn how to sensitively and appropriately stimulate the clitoris during lovemaking? Certainly not from their tongue-tied fathers, their boastful locker-room peers, high-school "health" classes, love scenes in literature, porno films, orgasm-faking prostitutes, and the vast majority of sex advice material.

No, the best place to learn how to make love is with a lover. And is there anything sweeter than a couple (safely) exploring and learning about sexual pleasure together? This is where a man can get the kind of honest, minute-by-minute feedback that will help him progress from bumbling ignorance to loving proficiency.

But communication barriers prevent many couples (even the most romantic) from making much progress in bed. Here's how one man described this dilemma as he and his first lover tried to figure out how to make love:

> Why didn't I just ask her some questions? Very few men are comfortable asking a woman what feels right for her, heightens her experience, and makes her climax. It seems to be something that men generally don't do.

Even if a man asks, the woman may be at a loss to explain to him what to do. A woman may know how to touch herself, but very few seem to know what a man can specifically do to excite her and make her come. Perhaps we fear that if we talk about it, the magic of the moment will go away. Well, not talking about it has created a situation that is not working for many people.

Unless men get specific and supportive under-the-sheets training from their partners, most will continue to be clumsy and ineffective and real gratification in the couple's sexual encounters is mostly one-sided (i.e., the man's). As the person on the losing side of this lopsided dynamic, a woman has the biggest incentive to speak up. But all too often she is disempowered and acts as a coconspirator with her sexually ignorant partner, a silent and unhappy enabler of lousy sex.

Among couples striving to make intercourse mutually satisfying, there's often talk about premature ejaculation—the man reaching his climax too early. In *Satisfaction*, Kim Cattrall writes, "Premature ejaculations were the bane of my existence for most of my adult sexual life. I felt used, frustrated, and unfulfilled."

> **Over the years, eager readers of even the most sophisticated sex manuals were getting** *exhortations, not explanations.*

This is a rare case of men being blamed (or blaming themselves) for unsatisfying intercourse. But the "fixes" often suggested for men—masturbating before heading out on a date, training the muscles to hold back ejaculation, squeezing the base of the penis just before orgasm, distracting oneself with nonerotic thoughts (baseball box scores, perhaps), or pulling out of the vagina—do not address the real problem. Since penis-in-vagina intercourse isn't producing an orgasm for most women, finding ways to keep the man thrusting for a longer period of time won't make things much better. Yes, it would be nice if the man could learn how to slow down and get his "hair trigger" under control (an especially difficult challenge for young men), but what these couples are really looking for is a way to stimulate the clitoris and bring the woman to orgasm as part of making love. Standard-issue intercourse, however long it lasts, will almost never accomplish this.

Some women don't have a problem speaking up in bed; they know exactly what they want sexually and have no hesitation in asking for it. But even when women do speak up, they are sometimes not heard. A liberated and assertive woman may tell her lover exactly what gives her pleasure, but there is a disturbing pattern: the man follows her directions for a short time but then reverts to what he was doing (or not doing) before she coached him. This seeming imperviousness to instruction was mentioned by a number of respondents in *The Hite Report* and puzzles many women. How can men be such bad listeners and such slow learners in bed? Is it *that* difficult?

In fairness to men, it's hard work *unlearning* our society's deeply ingrained idea of how sexual intercourse is supposed to work—which may explain why so many men keep "forgetting" the helpful pointers their braver partners give them. The accepted sexual script has a powerful, self-sustaining logic that has kept it alive from generation to generation. Rachel Maines describes the conventional wisdom as follows: the man and woman get aroused by kissing, caressing each other's bodies, and touching each other's genitals (foreplay); then the man puts his penis into the vagina (penetration); then, after some passionate thrusting, both partners reach the celestial heights (mutual orgasms). Maines calls this the androcentric paradigm. For the sake of clarity, let's call it the penetration-produces-female-orgasm model.

In light of what we know today, it's obvious why this model doesn't work. Because the clitoris receives only indirect stimulation (if that) when the penis is in the vagina, intercourse is one of the least effective ways for a woman to reach a climax—which is why in study after study, 65 to 85 percent of women report that they don't have orgasms during intercourse. These figures notwithstanding, many people—especially men—find it difficult to let go of the penetration-produces-female-orgasm myth. Why is this sexual script so persistent in the face of such well-documented evidence of its shortcomings? There are ten possible reasons:

1. It seems, well, *logical* that both men and women should reach orgasm together during the "main event," the procreative act. Why would Mother Nature have set things up for this not to be so?

2. Men tend to believe that what feels good for them must also feel good for their partner. And this belief is not as silly as it sounds. Until he is taught otherwise, a man tends to think of the vagina as a kind of inside-out penis, with the same sexual nerve endings on the inside that the penis has on the outside. From classical antiquity through the end of the seventeenth century, this is how most scientists thought of the female genitalia. With this mental picture, it's natural to think that penis-in-vagina intercourse will produce pleasure for the woman similar to what the man feels when his penis moves inside the vagina, and at the same pace.

3. The penetration-produces-female-orgasm paradigm has become deeply rooted in the male ego ("Don't worry, my penis can handle this job"). The belief is therefore stubborn and resistant to change. A man can become defensive—in fact, downright petulant—when a woman tells him that she isn't sexually satisfied by his passionate thrusting.

4. Not enough women speak up to correct men's misguided assumptions. This reticence may stem from

ignorance (Where is my clitoris, anyway?); from shyness (Will my sexual appetites shock him?); from shame (Will he think that I masturbate?); from insecurity (I'm not very good at this); from fear that there is something wrong with them (Am I frigid?); from a desire to appear worldly and mature (like in the movies); from fear of provoking jealousy (Will he think I've slept with other men?); from selflessness (It's too much to ask of him); from fear of seeming pushy (Will I come across as too demanding?); from fear of hurting his feelings (Will he hold this against me?); and from fear of losing the man (Will he dump me if I bring this up?).

5. The first few times a man has intercourse, his sexual attitudes are, relatively speaking, a *tabula rasa*. This is the ideal time for him to learn how to make love in a way that gives mutual satisfaction. But the beginning of a sexual relationship is also the time when a woman is *least* likely to take on the role of the teacher. She may be unsure of what she *should* be feeling during intercourse and worry that her partner is comparing her to other women he's slept with. In addition, the novelty and passionate intensity of first-time sexual encounters can keep a woman from tuning in to the finer points of lovemaking. It's all so exciting and hot and wet that she may not even *care* that she doesn't have an orgasm. These factors conspire with the other reasons for not speaking up to produce an unfortunate result: the teachable moments in early sexual

encounters often slip by without the man getting the feedback he needs to become a better lover.

6. Every time a woman fails to speak up about being unsatisfied with lovemaking, she inadvertently *trains* her partner in the correctness of the penetration-produces-female-orgasm model. This Pavlovian conditioning is further reinforced by the fact that basic intercourse is sexually satisfying for the man—he's rewarded with an orgasm. If nothing happens to provide negative reinforcement and suggest that there's more he needs to do, he's going to be increasingly convinced that sex this way is just fine.

7. Females have less physical, economic, and societal power in most relationships, and male perceptions therefore tend to rule. The more unequal a relationship is—the bigger the difference in age, wealth, self-assurance, and dependency in the man's favor—the less likely she is to rock the boat.

8. Societally-induced self-doubt, worries, and low self-esteem lead many women to blame themselves rather than their partners for unsatisfying sex. They are much more likely to think there is something wrong with them than to challenge the accepted model.

9. Sex scenes in movies and works of fiction often depict couples who have no trouble reaching peaks of passion during penis-in-vagina intercourse with no evidence of clitoral stimulation. Lady Chatterley reveled in

climaxing with her lover in the D.H. Lawrence classic
Lady Chatterley's Lover. The sexually insatiable Samantha
in *Sex and the City* moans and shouts ecstatically when
she makes love. And in *Forever*, Judy Blume's controver-
sial novel about a teenage girl's first love that became
must reading for every teenager when it came out in
1975, having an orgasm during intercourse sounds
pretty straightforward:

> This time Michael made it last much, much longer and I
> got so carried away I grabbed his backside with both
> hands, trying to push him deeper and deeper into me—
> and I spread my legs as far apart as I could—and I raised
> my hips off the bed—and I moved with him, again and
> again and again—and at last I came.

This scene has been read and reread countless times,
and it's fascinating. But like so many other fictional erotic
scenes, it adds nothing to our understanding of how
mutually satisfying lovemaking really works—and perpetuates the myths that leave us all fumbling in the dark.

10. No recognized authority in the field of sexuality
has come right out and said: "Now hear this: penis-in-
vagina intercourse rarely produces a female orgasm, and if
thrusting is all you do, you will forever miss out on
mutual satisfaction." Without a strong statement like this,
the other nine reasons continue to operate and each new

generation of lovers reinvents a one-sided way of making love.

And so it goes. A man might start out with the best intentions (it's a point of pride these days for a man to give his partner an orgasm), but communication in most bedrooms is so poor (and the available literature is so unhelpful) that few men escape their cluelessness. Some intrepid women take their lovers by the hand and give them helpful hints. But all too often, the man is defensive and inept, the woman gives up, and lovemaking ends without mutual satisfaction. The penetration-produces-female-orgasm myth lives on, and lovemaking continues to be, in the words of one woman quoted in *The Hite Report*, "an activity engaged in by two for the satisfaction of one."

> **Women who don't communicate their sexual needs are going to have to put up with clueless, unsatisfying lovemaking year after year.**

The sad truth is that for many women today, lovemaking isn't any better than it was for their great-great-grandmothers. In some ways, it may be *worse* because nowadays female pleasure is an expectation, some men are at least trying, and self-blame adds another layer of guilt and unhappiness. No wonder there are so many reports of sexual malaise and boredom.

Chapter Four

Faking It and Dealing with It

The third scenario among no-female-orgasm couples is when the woman *pretends* to have a climax during the penis-in-vagina part of intercourse. From the number of jokes in circulation ("Been faking it so long I forgot how it feels!") and some memorable episodes in movies (notably the restaurant scene in *When Harry Met Sally*), it's clear that faking sexual ecstasy happens a lot. Two recent surveys give us ballpark figures. A 1994 *Mademoiselle* study found that 69 percent of women admitted that they had faked an orgasm at least once. And a 1995 study by Celia Roberts found that almost all the women at one college said they pretended at least some of the time. (The success of this play-acting became apparent when men on the same campus were also surveyed; they said that the women they slept with *never* deceived them about having orgasms.)

> **Faked orgasms are bad news for women—and ultimately for men, as well.**

Looking for a silver lining, we might say there is some good news in these figures. If a woman feels called upon to pretend, it means that she believes her partner *cares* if she has an orgasm—and it shows that men have dispensed with whatever hang-ups their forefathers had about expressions of female sexual pleasure.

But faked orgasms are mostly bad news for women— and ultimately for men, as well. When a woman fails to be assertive about her own sexual needs, she deprives herself of deep pleasure, misses an opportunity to teach a man how her body works, perpetuates the penetration-produces-female-orgasm myth, creates unspoken tension and anger in the relationship, and gets herself into a bind from which it is difficult to escape. That's a lot of trouble from a little harmless fibbing.

So why do women do it? First, there is the *pressure* women feel from contemporary beliefs about the way sex is supposed to be. While Victorian women were brought up to think they *shouldn't* show sexual pleasure, modern women are led to believe that they *must*. Since Freud, notes Elisabeth Lloyd, orgasms during intercourse have become closely linked to women's "true womanliness and femininity," producing "enormous social pressure." Politically progressive women get the message that they have a God-given right to an orgasm when they make love. In fact, the word is out that a woman should have an orgasm (or multiple orgasms) *every time*. When *Sex and the City's*

Samantha climaxes ecstatically with lover after lover (look, Ma, no hands!), she is brainwashing every female viewer into thinking that it's all very straightforward, and if it's not happening to you, honey, you must be messed up. As recently as 1981, an American sex-advice book opined, "There is usually some psychological problem, however small or large, when a woman fails to climax with modest frequency during sex with a competent and likable lover."

There's also pressure on men. Locker-room wisdom is that if you don't give your partner an orgasm, you are unmanly, lousy in bed, and a failure as a lover. Men do not like to feel this way, and there's a strong tendency for them to put the ball right back into the woman's court, keeping the pressure on her.

A second reason for faked orgasms is when a woman senses that a desirable man is comparing her sexually to other women who don't seem to be having any trouble with unassisted climaxes during intercourse (they're probably faking, but who can tell?). A thirty-three-year-old man interviewed by *Glamour* in 1995 said, "When you find a woman who can come to orgasm through penetration and not just clitoral stimulation, keep her. She's a rare and wondrous thing." Attitudes like this can put sexually honest women at a competitive disadvantage in the dating marketplace. Female sexual pleasure is deeply arousing for most men, and when it's not present during lovemaking, men may be tempted to look elsewhere rather than work on improving their own skills. Women are keenly attuned to this dynamic, and if the couple does not have a reliable way to reach a sexual climax during intercourse, there's a strong temptation to try to make things right by providing a simulation of sexual ecstasy.

A third route to faking orgasms is more subtle. In the hotly romantic early weeks of a love affair, sheer physical attraction, pent-up desire, and novelty can create a very high level of arousal. A woman may enjoy the sex so much that she *sounds* as if she is having an orgasm—and may actually have one through sheer excitement and empathy with her part-

> **Sex with no orgasmic payoff—sex that consists of putting on an act for the benefit of a man—is not going to stand the test of time.**

ner's sexual pleasure. But as the relationship moves beyond the infatuation stage and sexual newness and excitement subside a little, the woman may experience less pleasure—but continue making orgasmic noises to please her partner and keep the magic alive. Over time, genuine enjoyment can segue imperceptibly into exaggerated pleasure and then into outright faking.

A fourth reason for faked orgasms is the fear many women have of bruising the male ego (an ego that is notoriously sensitive when it comes to sex) and losing the guy. As Betty Dodson says, "Women have been conditioned to sexually please men for food, shelter, and protection ever since we lived in caves." Whether a woman succumbs to this fear depends on her level of self-confidence and assertiveness and the power balance within a relationship. Some women can say with total honesty, "I've never faked an orgasm." They are willing to level with a man in bed, work on improving the sex, and let the chips fall where they may ("If he won't listen and can't learn, he's a jerk and I don't want him anyway").

But lots of other women are less sure of themselves, have less power within their relationships, and hesitate to speak up about unsatisfying sex. Rather than trying to correct ineffective lovemaking, they conclude that too much candor will hurt his feelings, insult his skill as a lover, jeopardize the relationship— or at the very least spoil the moment. As Stephanie Alexander wrote in *Cosmopolitan* in 1995, faking orgasms is "just a matter of expediency…When you have to get up for work the next morning, who has two spare hours to make him feel better about not making you feel great?"

So when the guy purrs, "Was it good for you, too, honey?" she's not very likely to say, "Actually, sweetie, I didn't come and, to tell you the truth, masturbation is a whole lot better than sex with you." As gravelly voiced Rosalind Russell sang in the classic musical, *Wonderful Town*, "That's a sure way to lose a man!"

A fifth cause of faking is when a man's attempts at foreplay are clumsy, unsatisfying, or even painful. The clitoris is a sensitive organ, and if foreplay is too rough, too rapid, too mechanical, or too intermittent, a woman can lose her place or get completely turned off. A super-goal-oriented man striving mightily to give his partner an orgasm can make a woman feel like a laboratory animal. In situations like this, the woman's highest priority may be getting done with intercourse as quickly as possible. Here is one woman's account from *The Hite Report*:

> When I come to the realization that I'm not going to reach orgasm, I fake one, so he'll stop rubbing the life out of my clitoris and get on to the business of coming and it will be over with. In order to teach him how to do it right would take a major education and psychotherapy job which is only worth going through with someone I really dig.

Couldn't a woman call for a time-out? Possibly, but that's tricky to handle and could be a relationship-ender. Faking at least keeps some options open.

A final reason for faking is when an empathetic man whose pleasure is closely tied to that of his partner cannot reach orgasm until she does—but isn't touching her in ways that are making hers happen. With an overabundance of generosity ("doing a favor for a friend"), a woman in this situation may pretend to come to help her struggling partner get over the top.

> **Trapped by men's expectations and unable to speak up about their own needs, many women convince themselves that faking orgasms is a good short-term strategy—but long term, it can cause major damage to a relationship.**

So there you have it: six ways that women can convince themselves that faking orgasms is a rational short-term strategy. The problem is that once they start, it's very difficult to stop. The longer a woman fakes and the more successful she is at deceiving her partner, the harder it is to tell the truth. Imagine his angry questions: "Why didn't you tell me earlier?! You've been doing this for *how* many years? What *else* have you been lying about?" So the orgasm-faker is trapped into continuing to breathe and moan and holler in ways that convince her partner that his penis has produced a major seismic event. And that lets even the most conscientious guy off the hook when it comes to giving his partner a *real* orgasm at some other point in their lovemaking session. "I'm done. She's done. Nighty-night." As he dozes off, his bad habits have been reinforced, his sexual ego has been falsely inflated ("What an amazing lover I am!"), the penetration-produces-female-orgasm myth has been kept alive, and another opportunity for honest feedback and real learning has been lost.

And honest guidance is what men need! The sad thing about the amusing and very well-acted orgasm-faking scene in *When Harry Met Sally* is that Sally actually appeared to be giving her imaginary lover directive feedback ("Oh God! Yeah, right there! Yes!"). She was, in fact, engaging in a triple deception: faking her own pleasure, faking giving helpful feedback, and faking that he was taking the feedback and doing the right thing for her. What a disaster!

The damage that ongoing faking does to a relationship is enormous. The woman often feels cheated, slighted, and angry—but her frustration and resentment are locked inside her own head because she can't talk to her mate about something very important that's bothering her. And whether she knows it or not, she is angry at herself for carrying on the charade. This is not a recipe for domestic happiness! Yet all too many women are caught up in the faking way of making love.

Sex with no orgasmic payoff—sex that consists of putting on an act for the benefit of a man—is not going to stand the test of time. It's likely to wither on the vine when the woman has reason to feel less friendly toward her partner, when she's angry about something, when she's not "in the mood." There can be other reasons, but resentment about not getting equal satisfaction in bed might be a prime cause for unhappiness with one's sex life—and for fending off a man's advances.

Happy Without Orgasms?

We've looked at three scenarios—Wham-Bam, Clueless, and Faking It—where couples have intercourse without the woman reaching orgasm. All these women are deeply unhappy with their sex lives, right? That seems like a no-brainer, but the reality is more complicated. In *The Hite Report*, 87 percent of the respondents said they *enjoyed* making love—this from a sample that, Hite's critics contend, was skewed toward feminist beliefs. And surprisingly, women who didn't have orgasms with their lovers were just as likely to say they enjoyed intercourse as those who did.

Shere Hite was so puzzled by these responses that she conducted a follow-up survey to get a better understanding of what the women were saying. From the responses (and other sources beyond Hite's work), it's clear that there are a number of emotional facets of intercourse that can make it truly enjoyable for a woman even if she doesn't have an orgasm. Here's what some women said:

- "It creates tender and intimate moments with a man."

- "The full body-to-body contact is as close as I can get to someone else."
- "It brings a spiritual dimension to our relationship."
- "It is a time when I have the man's undivided attention."
- "It is exciting and flattering to have my body give such pleasure to a man."
- "It is wonderful giving myself to him and having him appreciate that."
- "Intercourse makes me feel accepted, appreciated, affirmed, and loved."
- "It makes me feel competent, attractive, vital, whole, alive, and fulfilled."

Naomi, a woman quoted in *Our Bodies, Ourselves*, gave this thoughtful, nuanced description of her feelings about intercourse:

The times when I make love with Jonathan and I'm only a little turned on I enjoy hugging him. It feels good to be close with him. Do I feel maternal, sisterly, a friend? Maybe a need to be mothered? It's not sorted out, but I know I do feel good. It satisfies one of my needs—for joyous physical contact with another person—but it isn't really the intense sexual one.

In a sense, these women were agreeing with the old

saying, "When sex is good, it's the most beautiful thing in the world, but when sex is bad, it's still pretty good." What they are *not* saying is that intercourse gives them deep sexual gratification. Instead, they are thinking intimacy, spirituality, narcissism, and vicarious enjoyment of their partner's pleasure.

But we have to wonder: are these women *really* happy with intercourse—or have they settled for what they believe is attainable given the realities of their lives and their relationships? Is their lovemaking truly fulfilling—or have they done a cost-benefit analysis and resigned themselves to getting certain benefits that come from intercourse without the full measure of sexual satisfaction? In her follow-up analysis, Hite concluded that these women had indeed made these compromises and that this was the explanation for the counterintuitive 87 percent finding.

So are women in this category sexually happy? Yes, they are enjoying their love relationships. Yes, there are many positive aspects to sexual intercourse for them. And yes, it's possible to enjoy making love without having an orgasm. But like their Victorian counterparts, these women have lowered their expectations, given up on men as truly sensual lovers, and accepted that intercourse is not an arena for their own sexual fulfillment. For them, intercourse is a *portal* to other important aspects of life: security, intimacy, children, companionate love, and even domestic bliss.

This is not an irrational strategy and given the realities most women confront every day, it's nothing to sneer at. But this *modus vivendi* systematically deprives women of a core life experience—an experience that their mates are enjoying almost every time they make love.

As sexually satisfied men slumber blissfully after intercourse, it should not surprise us that some of these women masturbate to quench their built-up sexual desire with an orgasm. Over the centuries some women have done this; even in Catholic nineteenth century France it was an acknowledged phenomenon. Post-coital self-stimulation was specifically endorsed in an 1870 manual used by French priests hearing confessions: "If the husband should withdraw after ejaculation, before the wife has experienced orgasm, she may lawfully at once continue friction with her own hand, in order to attain relief."

For these women, both past and present, masturbation may be the continuation of a private sex life that has existed since childhood or adolescence. At some point, they discovered that they could give themselves a secret, wonderfully pleasurable sensation at absolutely no cost and without asking for help from anyone else! Through an efficient feedback loop—learning to touch themselves where it felt good and keeping going until it felt great—they found that having an orgasm was quite quick and easy—and felt amazing. At first, they may have believed they were the only person in the world who did this (I invented it!).

Masturbation is a less obvious discovery for girls than it is for boys, and first masturbation often takes longer for many girls to figure out. But once a girl (or woman) has given herself her first orgasm, the circuitry is connected for good, and subsequent orgasms become easier and increasingly pleasurable. Natalie Angier describes the process:

> The clitoris must be wired up to the brain—the big brain—before it can sing. The brain must learn to ride its little rod the way it must learn to balance its body on a bicycle. And once learned, the skill will not be forgotten. Some women learn how to climax in childhood, while others do not make the connection until adulthood. It is not an engineering problem, though. You can't figure it out with the neocortex alone...that thickly ruffled top layer of fish-gray tissue that cogitates, hesitates, and second-guesses every impulse. Instead you must tap into a more ancient neural locus, the hypothalamus, which sits on the floor of your brain...and reigns over appetite: for food, salt, power, sex.

As they get older, many girls who have discovered this private pleasure run into the widespread social taboo against masturbation and stop doing it or, if they continue, wrestle with feelings of shame and guilt. One woman quoted in *The Hite Report* put it this way:

> When you're young, you masturbate/touch yourself instinctually, then you stop when you hear it's "wrong" and "naughty," and then you try the rest of your life to get other people to touch you the same way, only they hardly ever do it right!

No wonder masturbation is common among women who are not fulfilled by intercourse (and sometimes by those who are). Some women masturbate with their fingers, others rub up against a pillow or sheets, others squeeze their thighs together, others use vibrators, and others use the stream of water from Jacuzzis or hand showers (a use that, for some reason, their designers don't advertise). For these women, masturbation is good clean fun without the interpersonal complications of making it happen during intercourse.

> Women who aren't sexually satisfied by intercourse sometimes see it as a portal to other sources of happiness, including security, intimacy, children, and even domestic bliss.

What about women who, for religious or personal reasons, are not comfortable with masturbation and are "pre-orgasmic" (a term coined by Lonnie Barback in *For Yourself*) when they have their first sexual relationship? Because they have never touched their genitals in a sexual way, they have only a vague sense of what produces pleasure, and this puts them at a disadvantage when they first have intercourse. This lack of self-knowledge means that they are less likely to communicate well with their partner (the same inhibitions that keep them from masturbating prevent them from speaking up), and they are unlikely to have orgasms during intercourse. A truly unfortunate lovemaking scenario is when a woman who has not learned how to give herself an orgasm goes to bed with a sexually inexperienced man. It's a case of the blind leading the blind, and the woman is almost certain to wind up sexually frustrated.

Nowadays, sexually unsatisfied women who don't masturbate can't set up a weekly appointment with a doctor for "vulvular massage" or take trips to a spa for "hydrotherapy." With no other outlet, they live without sexual gratification. Maybe they won't have symptoms of "hysteria," but there are likely to be other consequences within their intimate relationships. The frequency of intercourse with their partners might drop ("I'm too tired"), or sex might completely disappear from the relationship (the "sexless marriage").

Alternatively, women who are unsatisfied by intercourse might try increasingly exotic practices (anal sex, fisting, bondage, and sado-masochism, etc.); watch pornography (which is easier than ever to get on cable TV and the Internet, at video stores, and in hotel rooms—and don't worry, the movie title won't appear on your bill!); have an affair with another man (introducing novelty, the excitement of new love, and an element of danger); or have sex with another woman (from a realization of genuine lesbian or bisexual orientation—or frustration with the available guys).

But while these avenues might be helpful some of the time, they do not address the real problem—the basic anatomical difficulty of a woman getting deep sexual satisfaction from intercourse. The next two chapters return to this challenge.

Chapter Five

Simultaneous Orgasms: Are They Possible?

So far we have focused on sexual encounters where the woman does not have an orgasm while she is with her partner. What about women who *do* climax during intercourse? According to most surveys, as many as 35 percent of women are in this category. How are they and their partners managing to include female satisfaction in their lovemaking? What triggers these women's climaxes? And do they come simultaneously with their partners?

Freud's Wrong Turn

These questions lead us straight to the doorstep of Sigmund Freud, who had strong views on the subject. Beginning around 1905, Freud asserted that the clitoral orgasm, usually the result of masturbation, was an "infantile" precursor to the deeper, more satisfying vaginal orgasm, which was produced by the man's penis during intercourse. In his *New Introductory Lectures on*

Psychoanalysis, Freud wrote:

> In the phallic phase of the girl, the clitoris is the domi-
> nant erogenic zone. But it is not destined to remain
> so; with the change to femininity, the clitoris must give
> up to the vagina its sensitivity, and, with it, its impor-
> tance, either wholly or in part.

Note that Freud said that the clitoris *must* give up its sensitivity. He wasn't reporting on research, and he wasn't describing something he'd learned from his patients; he was telling women what *needed* to happen. What about women for whom this transition did not take place? Freud believed that something was wrong with them. In 1935, he wrote, "In those women who are sexually anaesthetic, as it is called, the clitoris has stubbornly retained this sensitivity." Freud even referred one colleague to the practice of genital mutilation practiced by the Nandi tribe in Africa, suggesting that when this tribe cut off girls' clitorises, they were not suppressing female pleasure but merely redirecting it to the vagina, its appropriate adult location.

Freud's theory, bolstered by his medical and psycho-analytic reputation, reinforced many people's gut-level belief in the penetration-produces-female-orgasm paradigm. If the vagina was the source of "mature" female pleasure, then the natural order of the universe was for couples to have orgasms *together* during penis-in-vagina intercourse with no clitoral stimulation. Freud's theory sent generations of scientists and laypeople off in exactly the wrong direction.

It wasn't until 1953 that Alfred Kinsey's book *Sexual Behavior of the Human Female* debunked Freud's notion of the vaginal orgasm. A decade later, researchers William Masters and Virginia Johnson solidified Kinsey's findings and restored the clitoris to its rightful place at the

> From the 1920s through the 1950s, sexologists aggressively pushed the idea that having simultaneous orgasms during intercourse was a virtual duty—but gave couples no help on how to make them happen.

center of female sexual response. The painstaking Masters and Johnson research (which included putting a tiny camera inside a transparent plastic penis to get the inside story on intercourse) proved beyond a shadow of doubt that virtually all female orgasms are *caused* by clitoral stimulation (direct or indirect) and *felt* in muscular contractions in the vagina (and more generally). Masters and Johnson also found that orgasms from direct clitoral stimulation were the most intense, producing stronger contraction spasms and more rapid heartbeats. Many of the women they interviewed reported that their best orgasms came from masturbation.

What about other female-orgasm-producing areas? Masters and Johnson found that a small number of women were capable of having orgasms from breast stimulation. In recent years, theories have been advanced about other parts of a woman's body—the area around the urethra, the cervix, the G-Spot, and the A-Spot. Are these competitors for the clitoris's top spot? Probably not. One explanation for the seeming proliferation of erogenous zones in the genital area is that the visible clitoris is just the tip of the iceberg: once aroused, its roots are activated and can be stimulated through contact with nearby areas. Natalie Angier describes this phenomenon with her usual panache:

> The clitoris overspills its anatomical borders and transcends its anatomy. Other pathways feed into it and are fed by it. The fifteen thousand pudendal nerve fibers that service the entire pelvis interact with the nerve bundles of the clitoris. That's why the anus is an erogenous zone. Nerves are like wolves and birds: if one starts crying, there goes the neighborhood.

But the clitoris is the center of the action. The consensus among sex researchers is that in almost all cases, the clitoris is the source of female orgasms. The best proof of this is to ask what part of the body virtually all girls and women stimulate when they masturbate. It's the clitoris.

So Freud was wrong about there being distinct clitoral and vaginal orgasms, wrong about vaginal penetration producing orgasms, wrong about clitoral orgasms being immature and inferior, and wrong in saying that women who don't climax through vaginal intercourse are disordered. How could he have been so far off so many bases?

Maybe we should cut the man some slack. After all, he was working with research methods that were primitive by our standards, and many of his Victorian contemporaries must have found it difficult to talk openly with him about sex. But Freud was a smart, well-informed scientist who could and should have done better. His theory of the vaginal orgasm had no basis in observation or empirical research and flew in the face of centuries of insight on the role of the clitoris in female satisfaction. Many Victorian medical books, numerous screeds warning against masturbation, and countless works of pornography made it clear that the clitoris was the source of the female orgasm. Freud was certainly aware of at least some of this material, yet he went right ahead and willed the vaginal orgasm into existence. What was he thinking? Here is sex scholar Thomas Laqueur's attempt to get inside Freud's head:

> Freud knew that the natural locus of a woman's erotic pleasure was the clitoris and that it competed with the

culturally necessary locus of her pleasure, the vagina…Whatever polymorphous perverse practices might have obtained in the distant past, or today among children and animals, the continuity of the species and the development of civilization depend on the adoption by women of their correct sexuality. For a woman to make the switch from clitoris to vagina is to accept the feminine role that only she can fill…to assure that bodies whose anatomies do not guarantee the dominance of heterosexual procreative sex nevertheless dedicate themselves to their assigned roles.

So here was yet another missed opportunity in the history of human sexual happiness. Freud understood the sexual asymmetry of men's and women's bodies and knew that sexual intercourse wasn't deeply satisfying for most women. He recognized the importance of the clitoris and the deep biological need for orgasms in both men and women ("hysteria" being the result when women were deprived of sexual satisfaction). And he had the intellect to solve the puzzle and the medical prestige to get helpful advice into the hands of generations of lovers.

Instead, he veered off in another direction. His deeply held patriarchal beliefs, as well as his irrational fear that humans would somehow stop copulating and civilization would come to an end without vaginal orgasms, led him to an astonishingly wrong-headed conclusion. Having confronted the awkward fact that vaginal intercourse wasn't working sexually for most women, he concluded that it *must* work! He unilaterally declared that clitoral pleasure should be abandoned or repressed at puberty so

> **Sex research in the 1960s and 1970s made clear that the clitoris was the source of virtually all female orgasms.**

that male desire would be heightened, heterosexual union would be cemented, and the future of family and civilization would be assured. In so doing, Freud ran roughshod over well-established medical knowledge, reinforced the penetration-produces-female-orgasm myth, led generations of couples away from lovemaking techniques that might have provided real satisfaction for women—and made it all the woman's fault if things didn't work out as he said they should. This was a profound disservice to the world's lovers.

Female Orgasms during Intercourse

When Kinsey and Masters and Johnson set the record straight on the true source of female orgasms, the time was right for people to rethink the mythology of vaginal orgasms and take a fresh look at how simultaneous orgasms really occurred (if they occurred at all).

But it was not to be. The persistence of the penetration-produces-female-orgasm paradigm—and a research quirk—prevented most people from taking the next logical step.

A little known fact about the Masters and Johnson study was that they deliberately recruited women who *said* they were able to climax during intercourse. This decision confused the issue and muddied their findings because it left ambiguous the question whether their orgasms were assisted by direct clitoral stimulation. If the clitoris was really the source of all orgasms, how were the women in the Masters and Johnson study able to have an orgasm during intercourse? Were they built differently? Did they use some special technique? Did their partners? The same question goes for all other women who report that they have orgasms with their partners during penis-in-vagina sex.

With these questions in mind, let's take a look at seven reasons that women might answer yes when asked if they have an orgasm during intercourse:

1. *Clitoral-hood stimulation.* When a woman is in the final stage of arousal (after plenty of foreplay), her labia are fully engorged and the penis thrusting in the

> **Clitoral-hood stimulation during intercourse has been described as a Rube Goldberg approach.**

vagina can pull the labia back and forth over the clitoral hood, stimulating the clitoris and theoretically producing an orgasm. Could this penis-to-labia-to-hood-to-clitoris stimulation be the way some women have orgasms during intercourse? Researchers have not been able to observe a climax taking place this way (it's quite difficult to film!), and there are real doubts about how it can work unless the woman has already begun her orgasm from direct clitoral stimulation prior to penetration. For this method to produce a no-hands orgasm for the woman, the man must continue thrusting vigorously all the way through his partner's orgasm—and this is *really* difficult because he's engaged in the activity most likely to give him a rapid orgasm—while she is likely to take even longer than usual because the clitoral stimulation is indirect. If the man comes before his partner, the clitoral-hood tugging is going to cease forthwith because most men don't like to continue thrusting after orgasm. Given these seemingly insurmountable pacing and timing challenges, it's no wonder that Shere Hite called this method "more like a Rube Goldberg scheme than a reliable way to orgasm." Clitoral-hood stimulation probably accounts for a very small percentage of during-intercourse orgasms, if any at all.

2. *Bumping the clitoris.* Because of the wide variety of human body shapes and dimensions, different men and

women fit together in a variety of ways during intercourse. In certain positions (notably female on top), some women are able to perform a back-and-forth or circular grinding motion that rubs the clitoris against the man's pubic bone or the base of his penis. This can produce an orgasm, and can even bring about simultaneous orgasms if the man is poised to climax when the woman reaches hers.

This technique works for some couples, but it was reported by a few women in *The Hite Report* to be distracting and unappealing to some men, who were put off by the woman's self-stimulating movements (it felt like she was masturbating *on* him) and preferred a more comfortable position. There are no reliable statistics on how many couples successfully use the clitoris-bumping approach, but it's unlikely to be a very large number—and their partners may not be happy campers.

3. *The G-spot.* This much-debated feature of female sexual anatomy was first noticed by Kinsey in the 1940s, officially discovered by a German doctor named Ernest Grafenberg in 1950, and popularized (and named after Grafenberg) by John Perry and Beverly Whipple in the 1980s. The G-spot is a sexually sensitive urethral sponge-like tissue that can be stimulated through the front wall of the vagina by rubbing with a "come hither" motion with one or two fingers. Firm and sustained G-spot stimulation can produce an

intense orgasm in about 10 percent of women, and G-spot orgasms are sometimes accompanied by an ejaculation of fluid through the urethra (the fluid is not urine and appears to be produced by the Skene's glands around the urethra).

A man's penis can stimulate the G-spot if it enters the vagina from behind at a shallow angle. But trying to have a G-Spot orgasm during intercourse is not easy, and it comes with the same challenges of pacing, timing, and sustaining stimulation as the two methods described just above; it's extremely difficult for the man to hit this spot just right and synchronize his own orgasm with his partner's. So the G-spot is not a reliable method for no-hands, during-intercourse orgasms, and it's not an option for the estimated 90 percent of women who do not respond with orgasm to stimulation in this area. In addition, women who use a diaphragm for birth control may not have access to their G-spot because the lower edge of the diaphragm covers it.

4. *Sheer-excitement orgasms.* In the hotly passionate early stages of a love affair, it's possible for a woman to have an orgasm more from mental than physical stimulation. After all, the brain is the body's most sensitive sexual organ; women, like men, can have orgasms in their sleep, so they can certainly have an orgasm if they are swept away with lust and novelty and vicarious excitement. But this kind of hands-free "vaginal"

orgasm is impossible to sustain after the steamy initial stages of a relationship. No couple can keep up this level of novelty and passion, so sheer-excitement orgasms don't stand the test of time.

5. *Orgasms with a small "o."* When questioned closely by researchers about their during-intercourse orgasms, some women say that what they are having is a mild or "emotional" orgasm without the intensity of a full, clitoris-driven climax. One of the women quoted in *The Hite Report* described it as "the boom of a distant explosion, powerful but somewhat muffled, versus the high, sweet, rippling sensation, the peak of sensitivity, with direct clitoral stimulation." Another Hite respondent wrote:

> I never have the same sort of violently physical orgasms with vaginal penetration with the penis as I do with direct clitoral stimulation. I'm not even sure if I come. I get a great sensation of pleasure, but it never peaks like it does the other way. I wish it did. I'd love to come right when he does without any extra attention.

Similarly, women who have never had an orgasm, either alone or with another person, can mistake a high level of arousal—reaching a pleasant plateau during intercourse—for a real orgasm. They might very well tell a sex researcher that they are having orgasms during lovemaking when in fact they aren't.

6. *Orgasms before or after penetration.* When a researcher inquires about orgasms during sexual intercourse, a woman may think she's being asked if she has an orgasm *at some point in the lovemaking encounter.* If her partner brings her to orgasm *before* penetration or *after* withdrawal, she might say, "Yes, I have an orgasm when I make love," giving researchers the impression that it happened while her partner's penis was in her vagina. This misunderstanding seems to have happened frequently in sex interviews and probably accounts for Kinsey's anomalous finding that three quarters of women said they had orgasms with their partners; Kinsey's subjects were apparently including "assisted" orgasms that happened before, during, and after

> Let's face it: because of the location of the clitoris, hands-free intercourse is not an efficient or effective way for a woman to have an orgasm.

penetration. We'll look at separate orgasms in the next chapter, but let's be clear: these are not "vaginal" orgasms.

7. *Fibbing.* As we saw in the discussion of faked orgasms, women are under a lot of pressure to buy into the penetration-produces-female-orgasm paradigm. Many feel that if they are not orgasmic during intercourse, something is wrong with them. If some women are capable of tricking their lovers into thinking they are

having an orgasm during penis-in-vagina intercourse, isn't it likely that they would continue the deception when interviewed by sex researchers? Why not?

Taken separately, each of these seven possibilities erodes the credibility of the perennial research finding that 15 to 35 percent of women have unassisted orgasms during penis-in-vagina intercourse. Taken together, they strongly suggest that the number is much lower. We won't have a definitive answer until much more rigorous research is done, but the real figure is probably much closer to zero. Women who don't have an orgasm during penis-in-vagina intercourse are the overwhelming majority. They are *normal*!

Let's face it: because of the location of the clitoris, hands-free intercourse is not an efficient or effective way for a woman to have an orgasm. A very small percentage of couples may be able to make the clitoral-hood or clitoris-bumping technique work, but for everyone else, unadorned intercourse will never be an arena for serious female satisfaction. Accepting that fact is the essential starting point for finding our way to more mutually satisfying lovemaking.

Simultaneous Orgasms—
An Idea That Just Won't Quit

These facts notwithstanding, the idea of a man and woman having orgasms together during intercourse has persisted. Starting in the late 1920s, sex researchers and sex manual writers relentlessly pushed the idea that orgasms should happen *at the same moment.* T. Van de Velde's widely read marriage manual, *Ideal Marriage* (published in the U.S. in 1926) said, "In normal and perfect coitus, mutual orgasm must be almost simultaneous. The usual procedure is that the man's ejaculation begins and sets the woman's acme of sensation in train at once." This, of course, was complete nonsense, but because an authoritative book said it was true, thousands of couples worked hard to make it happen—and concluded there was something wrong with them (or at least with the woman) when it didn't.

The simultaneous-orgasm juggernaut continued. In 1953, the Kinsey Institute proclaimed that simultaneity was the "maximum achievement which is possible in a sexual relationship." Postwar marriage manuals exhorted husbands to "find the man in the rowboat" (an attempt to give prudish readers a visual image of the clitoris nestled between the labia) and touted the simultaneous orgasm as a virtual duty. In one popular advice book, *Love without Fear,* Eustace Chesson wrote: "Success comes to those who consciously and deliberately will to achieve. Both partners should, in coitus, concentrate their full attention on one thing: the attainment of simultaneous orgasm." Small wonder that one commentator bemoaned the "sex as work" ethic of this era.

> **Many couples have not been able to escape the penetration-produces-female-orgasm myth, and one-sided sex continues to be the norm.**

Couples tried and tried, and when the earth didn't move (a phrase coined by Ernest Hemingway to describe a torrid, apparently simultaneous climax in *For Whom the Bell Tolls*, a popular novel during this era), they felt let down. Lovers were being exhorted to have simultaneous orgasms, but the manuals didn't tell them *how*. Once again, exhortations without explanations—a formula for female frustration and a reason for women to fake orgasms at the moment that their partners ejaculated.

Despite a high failure rate, the idea of simultaneous orgasms kept rolling. In the last few decades, three offbeat books and a cottage industry of sexual gizmos have suggested new and better ways for couples to synchronize their orgasms. All have tried to address the inherent challenges to making this happen: the seemingly mismatched pleasure geography of men's and women's bodies (i.e., the difficulty of sustained, sensitive, and appropriate clitoral stimulation during intercourse); the different pace of arousal for men and women during intercourse (with women usually taking longer to reach orgasm than men); and, of course, the deeply rooted penetration-produces-female-orgasm mind-set (which makes couples think that nothing "extra" should be necessary for a woman to climax during intercourse).

1. *Gizmos.* Many Internet sites and sexual catalogues tout an assortment of penile attachments designed to stimulate the clitoris during intercourse. At first blush, these seem like a good idea: the thrusting movements of the penis push the attachment against the clitoris, giving direct stimulation to the woman in just the right spot. But if the man is out in front of his partner on the road to orgasm (and he usually is), he has to slow down or stop to avoid coming before her—but this slows down or stops his device from stimulating her clitoris! Even if the gizmo vibrates (which some do), the positioning, pacing, and timing challenges are significant. In addition, a rubber or plastic attachment often fails to stimulate the clitoris in the sensitive way that's necessary for maximum pleasure. Finally, lots of couples are loath to buy and put on such attachments, believing that sexual pleasure should happen using only the equipment they were born with. So for all the marketing hype, penile attachments are far from being a surefire route to simultaneous orgasms.

2. *Triggering Techniques.* In their book, *Simultaneous Orgasm and Other Joys of Sexual Intimacy*, Michael Riskin and Anita Banker-Riskin touted the sublime experience of reaching orgasms together and described

a series of exercises, practice sessions, and triggering techniques for climaxing at the same moment. The Riskins report that this approach works for many couples, bringing a much higher level of mutual pleasure and togetherness than is possible with separate orgasms.

But the Riskins' techniques are almost never mentioned outside their own publications. The failure of their approach to sweep the nation is most likely due to two factors. First, the steps they describe are complicated, challenging, and time-consuming, which goes against a strong cultural belief that intercourse should be a spontaneous, unscripted, and instinctive act of love—in other words, good lovers should be able to perform well in bed without needing to follow an elaborate instruction manual. Second, many couples do not have the time and energy in their busy lives to implement this program on a regular basis; late on a Friday or Saturday night, they need a lovemaking approach that is quicker and less elaborate. The Riskins' approach works only for couples who don't mind following an involved script and have large blocks of private time for lovemaking. This is not a large demographic.

3. *The Tip Technique.* In her book *How to Satisfy a Woman Every Time*, Naura Hayden proposed a technique that seems much simpler. After some foreplay, the man rubs his partner's clitoris with the tip of his penis and then teases her by partially entering her vagina until she begins to have an orgasm, only then pro-

ceeding with his own. Hayden enthusiastically claims that her technique is virtually foolproof and that thousands of couples are using it successfully.

But there are real challenges to using this approach. First, the penis is a fairly blunt instrument for providing sensitive stimulation to the clitoris, and it can't do the job by itself (someone needs to take it by the hand); most people find that fingers or the tongue are more sensitive and therefore more effective at bringing a woman to orgasm. Second, Hayden doesn't say how the clitoris gets stimulated during the endgame when the penis is inside the vagina (and, as we have seen, continuous stimulation up to and during orgasm is essential to full satisfaction for a woman). The Hayden technique might work the first few times by dint of novelty and sheer excitement, but after that, many of the women using it may be secretly unsatisfied, settling for a milder "emotional" orgasm—or faking it.

4. *The Coital Alignment Technique (CAT)*. In their book *The Perfect Fit*, Edward Eichel and Philip Nobile gave a detailed description of what they called a revolutionary new technique. They said that CAT allowed up to three-quarters of the women in their study to have hands-free orgasms during intercourse, and that the frequency of simultaneous orgasms during intercourse increased from 5 percent to 50 percent of couples.

Here's how the Coital Alignment Technique works:

using the missionary position, with the woman's legs extended and wrapped around her partner's calves and the man's weight distributed evenly along her body, the man rides higher than usual and uses deep penetration so that his partner's clitoris is aligned with the base of his penis. The partners then use an up-and-down rocking motion that continuously stimulates the clitoris. One man quoted in *The Perfect Fit* described how his lover taught him CAT as they made love one day:

> In the middle of a basic thrust (I was on top), she suddenly grabbed my hips and whispered to me, "No, don't...slow down...stop." At first, of course, I panicked, imagining that perhaps we were back in the "rushing it" category, that I'd made some wrong, horrifyingly anti-erotic maneuver that signaled to Anne—"system shut down." Not the case! She grabbed me passionately, and as I looked at her, I could see that the expression on her face was not one of frustration, but of happiness and anticipation. She said, "Stop...just rock, so slow, so slow..." She grabbed me tightly, and then with her hands on my hips she guided the way she wanted me to go. She lifted me slightly higher so that my body was more acutely on top of hers. And as I tried to thrust (because I still didn't know exactly what she had in mind), she held me back. I was still inside her, but rather than pushing in and out, she led me into what I would

call almost sliding my shaft along her clitoris in a slow, rocking, almost circular motion. I could see on her face that this was deeply erotic to her, that, compared with the look on her face just a few moments before (traditional style), she was in another zone. Her head arched back, her eyes closed tight, she whispered to just keep doing that, doing that. In what seemed just a few seconds, she came. She came for what at the time felt like thirty or forty seconds, writhing and almost crying and even letting out a small yelp.

Another fan of the Coital Alignment Technique had this to say about how it affected her view of intercourse:

You realize that you can feel even more positive about your partner because this isn't something that somebody else *did* to you. You did this thing *together*. You don't think, this guy is *a great lover*. It's not just him—it's you, too! I think you feel better about the other person *because* it wasn't all him...Intercourse is more equitable.

Eichel and Nobile's book contains helpful diagrams and it all sounds and looks great. But once again, we have to be skeptical about a hands-free approach, however ingeniously choreographed, because of the challenges of pacing and timing. With the stimulation of the clitoris dependent on the man's thrusting movements, how can the man hold back his own orgasm while bringing his partner to hers? In addition, the CAT positions are somewhat awkward, and even Eichel concedes that "it requires considerable discipline to learn this motion."

So after the novelty has worn off, is CAT just one more attempt to make the penetration-produces-female-orgasm model work without solving the fundamental problem? It's not surprising that Em and Lo, the savvy, let's-try-anything online sex advice columnists, greeted the CAT with skepticism in their book, *The Big Bang*. Too difficult, too complicated, not worth the trouble, they said. Although there are no reliable statistics, it appears that the CAT is going the way of other simultaneous orgasm techniques: practiced successfully by a few, tried and abandoned by others, unknown to most.

The simultaneous orgasm approaches advocated by Eichel and Nobile, Hayden, and the Riskins (and the devices that stimulate the clitoris during intercourse), are all thoughtful, well-meaning attempts to address the challenge of mutual satisfaction during intercourse, and they all have their devotees. But none of them has succeeded in bringing about a major revival of the idea of synchronized orgasms. It appears that only a small minority of couples are using these techniques, and the conventional wisdom in the sex literature is now quite negative on simultaneous orgasms. A perusal of current articles, books, videos, and Internet sites on the subject of simultaneous orgasms reveals the following:

- An evasive silence. The unstated conclusion may be that simultaneous orgasms are physically impossible and not worth discussing—or perhaps some authors have yet to realize that penetration-produces-female-orgasm is a myth.

- Advice to chill out. Some counsel couples not to be so goal-oriented and genitally focused; women don't need to have orgasms to have a satisfying sex life, they say. Natalie Angier finds this as convincing as saying that some homeless people like living outdoors. Indeed, this argument sounds like a male rationalization for not making the extra effort to bring their partners to orgasm. Either way, this advice is a recipe for female frustration. Healthy adults have a built-in appetite for orgasms—an appetite that grows with each passing day and wants to be satisfied at regular intervals. Sure, there are times when one partner or the other is not able to have an orgasm due to fatigue, preoccupation, illness, etc. And yes, it's possible to enjoy intercourse without an earth-shattering orgasm. But with a little extra care and attention (details in the next chapter), orgasms can be part of lovemaking for *both* partners almost all of the time, satisfying the man's *and* the woman's emotional and biological needs as part of one conjugal act.

- Too difficult and not worth striving for. In 1990, the Kinsey Institute changed its position, declaring that simultaneous orgasms were not an important part of marital happiness—or even a desirable goal. Why frustrate people, the Institute argued, when men can't control their orgasms and women can't either? Around the same time, Masters and Johnson wrote that a simultaneous orgasm is a lovely thing when it happens, but to try for it deliberately would be an "imposition of technique." Lou Paget, a sex book author, has this advice for men: "So, gentlemen, do not feel inadequate if simultaneous orgasm is not part of your repertoire."

- Too limiting. In his sexual autobiography, Richard Rhodes wrote: "Single-mindedly pursuing orgasm, particularly a will-o'-the-wisp like mutual simultaneous orgasms, narrow[s] and limit[s] pleasure."

- A bad thing. Most recent sex literature is flat-out critical of the idea of simultaneous orgasms. Here is a sampler:
    - Helen Singer Kaplan says "the myth of the mutual orgasm is the most destructive heterosexual myth in American society."
    - Stefan Betchell and his colleagues believe that striving to synchronize orgasms is a

turn-off because it constantly pressures the woman to hurry up and the man to slow down.

- Michael Castleman says that trying to have orgasms together is like asking all the people at a banquet to eat their last bite at exactly the same moment.

- Dr. Clifford and Joyce Penner approvingly quote a woman who said, "I wouldn't want to orgasm when he does because then I would miss out on his."

- Perhaps the most dismissive attack is in *The Big Bang*, a comprehensive sex advice book by Emma Taylor and Lorelei Sharkey: "***How to Achieve Simultaneous Orgasms During Penetration Every Time:*** We have no idea."

The critics of simultaneous orgasms have what seems like an airtight case. The challenge of simultaneous orgasms is similar to the difficulty of the "69" position—fellatio and cunnilingus performed simultaneously. In "69", each person is stimulating the other's genitals in a way that should produce an orgasm, but each is proceeding at a different pace, and both partners have to communicate (without being able to speak very easily!) and coordinate their timing (usually by slowing down the man's pace) so they can reach orgasm at the same

> **Despite occasional attempts to revive the idea, the prevailing wisdom in today's sex literature is that simultaneous orgasms are neither possible nor desirable.**

moment. It's easy for a sixty-niner to get caught up in his or her own orgasm and stop stimulating their partner—or lose their own place while concentrating on pleasuring their partner. The difficulty of getting the timing right is the reason that "69" is talked about more than it's practiced. Too complicated! Too much like juggling!

Achieving a simultaneous orgasm during penis-in-vagina intercourse would seem to pose equally daunting challenges:

• It's not a simple matter to sensitively stimulate a woman's clitoris during actual intercourse.

  • It's not easy for two people to synchronize the pacing; if the woman feels pressured to rush her orgasm and the man feels he must put on the brakes, intercourse is less enjoyable.

  • It's difficult to do two things at once—kind of like trying to rub your tummy and pat your head simultaneously.

  • Because both the penis and the clitoris become very sensitive to touch right after orgasm, there is a narrow window of time (less than a minute) within which simultaneous orgasms must occur to get the full benefit; after that, most people don't want their most sensitive spot touched for a while.

• The intensity of your partner's orgasm can distract you from enjoying your own, and grooving on your own orgasm can distract you from enjoying your partner's.

Because of these hurdles, it certainly seems that the idea of simultaneous orgasms during intercourse, once thought to be essential to procreation and the essence of successful lovemaking, is not a winner.

So as the difficulty of mutual orgasms during intercourse has sunk in over the years, and as women have increasingly spoken up about being shortchanged by intercourse ("Honey, you were great, but I haven't come yet"), there's been a grudging acceptance (at least by some) that penetration doesn't produce female orgasms—and that simultaneous orgasms are virtually impossible.

If this is true, what are lovers who want to share sexual satisfaction during lovemaking supposed to do? The next chapter tackles this question head-on.

Chapter Six

Three Approaches to Mutual Satisfaction

By trial and error and good communication, some couples have found their way to three quite different approaches to mutual satisfaction. Each has advantages and disadvantages, all require compromises from the conventional paradigm for intercourse, and none is perfect for everyone. But all three have the virtue of successfully clearing the hurdles to mutual gratification and giving both lovers orgasms within a lovemaking session. For the second and third approaches, the orgasms can be virtually simultaneous. This chapter describes these approaches in some detail.

> **With little or no help from sex-advice literature, some couples have found their way to three effective techniques that allow both partners to have orgasms during a lovemaking session.**

1. Separate Orgasms

The first approach seems obvious, yet is almost never mentioned explicitly in the historical or contemporary sex literature: the woman has her orgasm *before or after* the penis-in-vagina part of lovemaking. Couples who take this approach to mutual satisfaction have faced reality and defied the strong cultural expectation that female orgasms should happen *during* intercourse. They have created a new protocol for making love: first you, then me. With an ironic tip of the hat to the Civil Rights struggle, one commentator dubbed this the "separate but equal" approach to orgasms, giving it a contemporary ring, but it has almost certainly been used by some couples through the ages.

For some couples, having separate orgasms becomes a mainstay, and it can work wonderfully well. Each person is able to concentrate on the pleasure of his or her own orgasm and then revel vicariously in the partner's orgasm (or orgasms) a few minutes later. In the words of one man who swears by this approach:

> I love—LOVE—to have an orgasm that is all my own. I also love having my wife come all on her own—and she loves it, too—in a way that is full of abandon and completely focused on her own pleasure, and on my making her pleasure.

For lovers who have separate orgasms, the man's is usually—but not always—in his partner's vagina. The woman's orgasms can be triggered in a variety of ways—oral stimulation (a favorite for some women but not for others), manual stimulation, vibrators, or other sex toys. There's an array of choices, and some couples vary their selections from one lovemaking session to another. Others settle down to a regular routine once they have found what works for them.

Afterward, the lovers might hold each other, nuzzle, cuddle, lie back (still touching), and bask in the post-coital afterglow, perhaps dozing off together. After-play can be the most sweetly affectionate part of sex, and is accentuated when both partners are genuinely satisfied and have the same mellow, sexy, bonded feeling. In the words of Richard Rhodes:

> Is there anything on this earth finer than two human beings turned to each other in a comfortable bed, one's leg thrown over the other's hip, looking into each other's eyes, sharing the dawning day?

Couples who have separate orgasms often develop a protocol for taking turns. There are advantages to each possible sequence: if it's "ladies first," there's a gentlemanly feel to it and plenty of lubrication when it's time for him to enter the vagina. (In *She Comes First: A Thinking Man's*

Guide to Pleasuring a Woman, Ian Kerner explores the full potential for oral sex to bring the woman to orgasm before her partner.) For women who are capable of multiple orgasms (about 10 percent are believed to be in this category), the heightened arousal of having just had an orgasm may trigger additional orgasms during or after penetration. If the man comes first, there's some added lubrication from his semen (provided the couple is not relying on condoms for birth control and disease prevention) and a less rushed feeling for the woman. Either way can be great.

> **Having separate orgasms (first you, then me) is a breakthrough for many couples, introducing an unhurried, mutually satisfying dynamic to their sexual relationship.**

Compared to one-sided 3-2-1 sex and female faking, the separate-orgasms approach is a huge step forward. Both partners are having orgasms within a single lovemaking episode, there's much more of a feeling of sharing and mutuality, and there's real equality between the lovers. Women are the biggest beneficiaries: if they are getting genuine fulfillment from making love, they are much more likely to be happy with the sexual relationship (no more faking, no more resentment, and little need for masturbation).

Men are winners, too: consciously or unconsciously,

most of them know that lovemaking is better for their partners and get deeper satisfaction and enjoyment as a result. These feelings can ripple out into other parts of the relationship, contributing to a more good-natured, sharing dynamic. Mutual satisfaction in bed is no cure-all if a relationship has deep problems, but for people who have a solid love relationship, it defi-

> **Shere Hite reported that some women reach down and touch their own clitoris during penis-in-vagina intercourse, but this approach is rarely mentioned in today's sex literature.**

nitely helps with everyday stresses—in addition to adding measurably to the enjoyment of life.

For a woman sizing up a man, there is one additional advantage in the separate-orgasms approach. A man reveals a lot about himself in bed, and the asymmetrical design of men's and women's bodies poses a test that self-centered, insensitive, and unscrupulous men are likely to flunk. Looking back on a lovemaking encounter, a woman can ask herself: Is he gentle and passionate? Does he care about my sexual needs? Is he willing to take the time to learn how my body works? Does he listen to me when I tell him what I like, or does he follow a set script (probably the same one he uses with every other woman he sleeps with)? Does he use a condom and protect me from pregnancy and disease? And does he make the extra effort and exercise the mature restraint to make sure I'm satisfied before he goes to sleep? In short, is he a good potential mate—or is he a jerk?

For some couples, separate orgasms are wonderful—even sublime—and taking turns is their top choice of any possible lovemaking approach (including the other two in this chapter). But other lovers are less enthusiastic. They can't get the penetration-produces-female-orgasm model out of their heads and aren't willing to make the compromises involved in having separate orgasms. A man in this category may have a grudging attitude as he gives his partner her orgasm. One angry guy quoted in *Our Bodies, Ourselves* exclaimed, "I do half the housework, half the child care, and now half of this. This is going too far!"

> **The least-mentioned approach to mutual orgasms is the man caressing his partner's clitoris during intercourse and holding off his own orgasm until she begins hers.**

The Hite Report also picked up on this undercurrent of impatience and resentment: it was clear that some men felt it was a burden and a chore and wished the woman could have her orgasms vaginally without all the extra *work*. Sex researcher Alexander Lowen's book *Love and Orgasm* further documented this male grumbling:

Most men feel that the need to bring a woman to climax through clitoral stimulation is a burden. If it is done before intercourse but after the man is excited and ready to penetrate, it imposes a restraint upon his natural desire for closeness and intimacy. Not only does he lose some of his excitation through this delay, but the subsequent act of coitus is deprived of its mutual quality...The need to bring a woman to climax through clitoral stimulation after the act of intercourse has been completed and the man has reached climax is burdensome since it prevents him from enjoying the relaxation and peace which are the rewards of sexuality. Most men to whom I have spoken who engaged in this process resented it.

And it's not just men who are ambivalent about separate orgasms. Here is the way a young woman put it in *Our Bodies, Ourselves*:

I have trouble asking that Jonathan continue to stimulate me after he has had an orgasm. It's hard for me to stay excited. I can't explain why because I haven't figured it out yet. Maybe I'm too self-conscious and not able to lose myself in my feelings. Also, part of what I find exciting is Jonathan's excitement and that is gone at that point...Sometimes we make love so that I have an orgasm before he enters my vagina. That's not bad,

> though I wish I could have one more with his penis
> inside me. The other way is a lot like masturbation and I
> feel I can do it better myself.

Not all couples have these misgivings; many are perfectly content with the compromises needed to make separate orgasms work. A strong love relationship, maturity, patience, and good communication are key requirements. If lovers really care about mutual pleasure, if they can talk about what they like and don't like, and if the other alternatives don't satisfy their needs, they can find a way to make first you, then me work well.

2. The Woman Touches Herself during Intercourse

In *The Hite Report,* Shere Hite proposed a different approach—one that makes it possible for a couple to have simultaneous orgasms during intercourse. Based on the responses of almost two thousand women to her in-depth sex questionnaire, Hite concluded that the only reliable way for a woman to have an orgasm during penis-in-vagina intercourse is to take care of it herself. The most direct version of the Hite approach is for the woman to reach down during intercourse and stimulate her clitoris with her own fingers (or with a vibrator).

This approach made an appearance in a memorable lovemaking scene in John Updike's 1968 novel, *Couples*:

He lost himself to the hilt unresisted. The keenness of her chemistry made him whimper. Always the problem with their sex had been that he found her too rich to manipulate. She touched his matted chest, *wait*, and touched her own self, and mixed with her fluttering fingers, coming like a comet's dribble, he waited until her hand flew to his buttocks and, urging him to kill her, she gasped and absolved herself from tension. He said, "My dear wife. What a nice surprise." She shrugged, flat on her back on the sweated sheet, her bare shoulders polished by starlight. "I get hot too."

And from *The Hite Report* itself, here is a woman's account of how she discovered this approach:

I was not *ever* having any orgasms all through four years of college and was *mortified* and thought something was terribly wrong with me. I could masturbate to orgasm *very* easily but couldn't feel a damned thing during intercourse. Well, I was with my long-standing boyfriend one day and we were making love and I got really pissed at my not having orgasms so, with him in me and moving, I just reached down, rubbed around my clitoris and decided that, by God, I was going to get off, and one to two minutes later, I sure did—I had a fantastic orgasm, and have been successful ever since, *every* time, by using this method!

This approach seems to have been discovered independently by some couples over time, and some lovers (we don't know how many) find it a wonderful way to make love. It puts the woman in the driver's seat on the road to sexual satisfaction and deals successfully with the challenges of body geography and timing. A variation is for the woman to stimulate her clitoris while her partner's penis is in her vagina, bring herself to the brink of orgasm, and then use the indirect stimulation of the man's final thrusting, or bumping the clitoris against the man's pubic bone, to put herself over the top. Hite endorses any approach in which women are the agents of their own orgasms—although she is skeptical about how well some of these techniques work (recall her characterization of clitoral-hood tugging as a "Rube Goldberg" method).

> **Any approach that brings both partners to orgasm has a huge payoff in the quality of lovemaking, how lovers feel immediately afterward, and the long-term viability of their sexual relationship.**

Natalie Angier was thinking along the same lines as Hite when she tried to make sense of the design and placement of the clitoris:

> In my view, all the intricacies we've been mulling—the apparent fickleness and mulishness of the clitoris, its asynchronicity with male responsiveness, and the variety of its performance from one woman to the next—can be explained by making a simple assumption: that the clitoris is designed to encourage its bearer to take control of her own sexuality.

Angier goes on to cite anthropologist Helen Fisher, who has found that women who have orgasms during intercourse "have one trait in common: they take responsibility for their pleasure. They don't depend on the skillfulness or mind-reading abilities of their lovers to get what they want. They know which positions and angles work best for them, and they negotiate said positions verbally and kinesthetically."

The Hite approach has real advantages for both partners. Because a woman's orgasm is powerfully arousing to a man when his penis is in his partner's vagina, his orgasm is likely to explode at the same time or shortly after his partner's. This means that couples who use the female-self-stimulation approach get all the benefits of simultaneous orgasms that have been written about (but seldom consummated) over the years. Some couples find that mutual orgasms are synergistic—the peak of pleasure and togetherness is equal to more than the sum of two separate orgasms.

The biggest advantages are for the woman. The vagina is not without sensation, and combining clitoral and vaginal stimulation—and at the same time feeling and hearing her partner's enjoyment and excitement so closely linked to her own—can accelerate a woman's arousal and heighten the intensity of her orgasm. Having an orgasm together, her vagina hugging her lover's penis, can make the climax more centered and more intense, literally giving her something to grab hold of. Since a woman's orgasm is partly expressed in vaginal contractions, having the penis thrusting inside her during her orgasm can produce an added dimension of pleasure, setting off an empathetic ricocheting of feelings back and forth between the lovers. Deep penetration during intercourse can also stimulate other erogenous areas and make for a more intense climax.

And there is a payoff for the man, too. He hears his partner's genuine enjoyment and may feel the strong vaginal contractions that accompany her orgasm. All this enhances the intensity of his own orgasm and can give him profound sexual and emotional gratification. If the man is having an off day and is having difficulty reaching orgasm, his partner's climax can mentally and physically put him over the top.

These are significant advantages, and there are clearly couples who are enjoying them on a regular basis. But despite the fact that *The Hite Report* has sold millions of copies and is still available today, and despite Natalie Angier's erudite support of Hite's basic conclusion, the woman-stimulates-clitoris-during-intercourse approach is almost never mentioned in current sex-advice material or popular culture. There are a number of possible reasons:

- Some people continue to have hang-ups about masturbation, and the Hite approach may turn off one or both partners.
- Even among lovers who are comfortable with masturbation, there may be a feeling that intercourse is not the time or place for it (the penetration-produces-female-orgasm myth strikes again).
- Some men (perhaps chauvinistically, perhaps generously) want to be the one who makes the woman's orgasm happen and think that if she is taking care of her own pleasure, he is not doing his job.
- Other men may believe that if the woman is doing her own clitoral stimulation, she is implicitly criticizing his efforts (which, if he is bumbling and inept, may in fact be true).
- There's also the feeling among some men that if the woman is stimulating her clitoris, he's no longer in touch with his partner's orgasm, which deprives him of what can be a wonderful part of making love—the pleasure of giving pleasure. When a man caresses his partner's clitoris through to orgasm, it is a tangible expression of love; it's also powerfully arousing.

- Finally, a couple using the Hite approach may feel that they are pleasuring themselves without *connecting* in a deeply mutual way. A *New Yorker* cartoon picked up on this feeling: a woman sits up in bed and says to her partner, "I feel we haven't moved beyond parallel play." (Of course this lonely feeling can occur with any approach where partners feel they are pursuing their own orgasms without a close emotional bond.)

For these reasons, the female self-stimulation approach seems to appeal to a fairly narrow demographic and has not made its way into the sexual mainstream. This is a shame, because it is one of the very few techniques that reliably gives a woman an orgasm during intercourse and can easily produce simultaneous orgasms.

3. The Man Stimulates the Clitoris during Intercourse

The Hite approach may lead some men to ask, "If she can do it, why can't I?" This may be one way that a small number of couples have found their way to the third and least talked-about approach to mutual orgasms: the man stimulating the clitoris during actual intercourse.

Judith Silverstein mentioned this technique briefly in her 1978 book, *Sexual Enhancement for Women*, and several women who contributed to *The Hite*

Report described it in passing. Only one book in the vast sex literature goes into any detail: Betty Dodson's *Orgasms for Two: the Joy of Partnersex*. But this book has received very little attention, and the man-stimulates-clitoris-during-intercourse technique is one that many couples may never have heard about or considered. This is unfortunate, because this approach—we might call it the great sex secret—can work wonderfully well.

The invisibility of this seemingly obvious mutual-orgasm technique is baffling. In the highly explicit pages of *The Joy of Sex* and other pictorial guides to lovemaking, and in countless sex scenes in movies and instructional videos, we virtually never see a man touching a woman's clitoris during penis-in-vagina intercourse. Even Chakrasamvara, a late-fourteenth-century Buddhist deity who is often portrayed making love in a sitting position with his twelve arms entwining his consort, doesn't use *one* of his hands to touch his partner's clitoris.

Is there a silent taboo at work here? It's as if men are responding to a powerful, unspoken prohibition and are programmed to keep their elbows on the mattress and their hands on the woman's shoulders or face or head or buttocks—anywhere but the clitoris. Okay, it's partly a matter of female geography—it would be a lot easier to stimulate the clitoris during intercourse if it were located, say, on one of her earlobes. But it may also be the result of the stubbornly resilient penetration-produces-female-orgasm paradigm: clitoral stimulation is reserved for *foreplay* and should not be necessary during intercourse.

But it *is* necessary. For couples who want to have orgasms together (and don't like the no-hands approaches described in Chapter 5 or the woman-touches-her-clitoris technique suggested by Shere Hite), having the man stimulate the clitoris while his penis is in the vagina is a reliable, straightforward way to bring a woman to orgasm. It's also a way to orchestrate simultaneous orgasms. Here's a step-by-step description of how it works:

- Foreplay proceeds as usual, with selections from the menu of kissing, touching, short-of-orgasm oral sex by one or both partners, and other positions and activities that allow the lovers to express affection, enjoy each others' bodies, and get thoroughly aroused.
- The man puts his penis into the vagina and does some gentle thrusting (not to orgasm) while continuing to kiss and caress.
- Then the man, with his penis still in the vagina, shifts his weight to one side, reaches down, and begins to caress the clitoris with his fingers. Staying tuned to his partner's level of arousal (communicated by her words, her sighs, her breathing, and

her body's response), and moving his penis just enough to keep himself on a plateau of arousal short of orgasm, he brings her closer and closer to her own. Depending on the time available and the lovers' energy level, they may want to approach orgasm one or more times and then back off and enjoy more mutual pleasuring before the finale.

- As the woman's orgasm begins, the man starts thrusting in earnest and flattens his hand against her belly, bearing down and continuing to rub the clitoris in a slower rhythm, following his own movements and hers, bringing her orgasm to its crescendo at about the same moment he reaches his own. Since a man's orgasm is usually shorter in duration than a woman's (about five seconds versus about twenty), it is possible for his to be entirely enveloped by hers, or it may happen just as hers finishes (allowing him to take his hand away for his final spasms), or it may arrive a few seconds after hers. The definition of "simultaneous" is somewhat loose; orgasms that occur within a minute of each other are close enough to reap the rewards.

- The couple lies back, one leg perhaps draped over the other's leg, a hand on a thigh, endorphins coursing their bodies, loving the mutual glow— and loving each other.

This little-known approach to mutual satisfaction during intercourse raises a number of questions:

Does making love this way require unusual skill? For it to work, four elements need to be present, none of which is out of reach for most mature, loving couples:

1. The man has to be willing to defer the primal thrusting of standard-issue intercourse and engage in a more restrained and nuanced approach choreographed with his partner's pleasure.

2. The man has to have the self-awareness and self-control to move his penis in the vagina just enough to keep himself aroused, but not so much that he has an orgasm before his partner (this is no small feat, especially for young, highly aroused lovers).

3. The man has to be able to stimulate the clitoris in a way that brings his partner to orgasm. There's no one right way to do this, and his skill depends entirely on feedback from his partner on what feels good and what doesn't.

4. Finally, the woman has to give *honest* feedback (usually nonverbal) on where she is on the road to orgasm so that her partner can match his own level of arousal to hers and join her when she comes.

Not all people are willing and/or able to exercise this level of empathy, communication, and restraint. The novelist Paul Coelho once wrote, "The art of sex is the art of controlled abandon," and not all couples are willing to exercise this type of control in the middle of sexual abandon. Couples who aren't—and those who don't find this approach appealing—will choose a different one.

Even if all four ingredients are solidly in place, the man-stimulates-clitoris-during-intercourse approach doesn't work 100 percent of the time. There are days when the man's timing is off and he has his orgasm before the woman reaches hers. And there are days when one partner is less easily aroused, has a muted climax, or is unable to have an orgasm at all (this, of course, is true for any approach to lovemaking). But most of the time, the man-stimulates-clitoris-during-intercourse approach is highly reliable.

Isn't it difficult for the man to reach the clitoris during intercourse? The main barrier is attitudinal, not physical. Once a couple has decided that touching the clitoris is an alright thing to do during intercourse, the body positions can be figured out. A man does not need to be a contortionist to pull this off; in fact, he can reach the clitoris in virtually all lovemaking positions—man on top, woman on top, sitting, entering the vagina from behind, even standing up—and he can reach it from the front or by reaching around from behind.

How about the problem of pacing—not feeling rushed or held back? The man-stimulates-clitoris-during-intercourse approach basically gets the man up onto a pleasant plateau of arousal, poised for orgasm, while the woman is brought toward orgasm at her own pace. There's no hurry (in fact, prolonging this phase can heighten the eventual orgasms), so she doesn't need to feel rushed and he (provided he has good self-control) can enjoy his plateau as he brings her along.

How about being distracted by the other person's orgasm? The man-stimulates-clitoris-during-intercourse approach is less of an awkward juggling of tasks than lovers experience in "69": the positions are more conventional, and only the man is doing two things, both of which connect him to mutual pleasure: his fingers keep him in touch with his partner's arousal while the walls of her vagina keep his penis in touch with his own arousal. The woman can relax and focus on her increasing arousal and the feeling of her partner's penis inside her, and her hands are free to hold and caress his back, buttocks, thighs, testicles, and penis. When the moment comes, it's possible for both partners to revel in their own orgasms, enjoy their partner's pleasure, and have their own pleasure enhanced by their partner's. Synergy is a definite possibility, as it is with the Hite approach.

Might some women feel this approach is too male-orchestrated? Women who want to be in control of their own pleasure are likely to have this reaction, in which case they'll want to use the Hite self-stimulation approach. But other women have no problem with their partner choreographing both orgasms. In fact, many women might find it a refreshing change for the man to take such an active role in giving her satisfaction, while at the same time her vagina is pleasuring him and bringing him to orgasm. This "division of labor" is as equal as the separate-orgasms approach; it avoids the resentment that comes when one partner feels that he or she is doing more "work" than the other, or has to concentrate on the partner's pleasure at a time when it would be nice to bask in the orgasmic afterglow.

Is this approach worth the trouble? For couples who find they can make it work, absolutely. All the advantages of having simultaneous orgasms that were described with the Hite approach apply here as well.

Why isn't the man-stimulates-clitoris-during-intercourse approach out there in the literature? That's a good question. Some couples have figured it out on their own, and it's probably been used by a small percentage of lovers going back hundreds or even thousands of years. But in historical and contemporary sex literature, it's truly the stealth approach to making love: the authors of countless books, articles, websites, and films do not mention it.

Why haven't the couples who use this approach written articles or books? Maybe they chanced upon it with a lover and didn't think of it as a sexual breakthrough.

(There's anecdotal evidence that couples tend to stumble upon this approach several years into a sexual relationship.) Maybe they assume that everyone makes love this way, so what's the big deal? Maybe they have a lingering feeling that this approach is a makeshift workaround and not the way intercourse is really *supposed* to work. Maybe they are shy and believe that the way people make love is a private matter that shouldn't be discussed outside the bedroom. Maybe they are not the type of people who write about sex and don't feel it's their job to spread the method they discovered. Or maybe they feel they would come across as boastful and presumptuous if they wrote about a sex technique that was working for them.

Whatever the reason, it's a shame that the man-stimulates-clitoris-during-intercourse approach is discussed so little. It is one of the very few ways to bring about mutual satisfaction during orgasm, and it can reliably produce simultaneous orgasms. As such, it deserves a place of honor on the sexual menu.

Each of the techniques described in this chapter solves the ancient riddle and brings mutual satisfaction within any couple's grasp. For couples who may have concluded that orgasms for both partners during lovemaking were impossible or just too complicated, these three approaches provide viable options. What we don't know is how many couples are using them. Elisabeth Lloyd wrote that because researchers haven't been asking the right questions, there is a dearth of information on how widespread "assisted" female orgasms during intercourse are across cultures.

Each technique has advantages and disadvantages. There are differences in the male skill level required (the Hite approach demands the least); in couples' desire

> **It is baffling that three viable mutual-orgasm techniques are almost never discussed in sex literature.**

for separate or simultaneous orgasms; in whether partners prefer to be in control of their own and their partner's orgasms; and in the compromises required by one or both partners from straightforward, way-it's-supposed-to-be intercourse. The key is exploring the *full* range of options (perhaps including some from Chapter 5 and some that haven't been written about yet), communicating honestly, speaking up if an approach is uncomfortable or a turn-off, and finding the one (or ones) that work best over time. Couples who make this journey and find what they're looking for are on the road to sexual happiness.

Chapter Seven

What's Technique Got to Do with It?

So far we've focused almost exclusively on the physiology of intercourse—what is usually called sexual technique. All this begs the question of what even the best lovemaking methodology has to do with love and romance. This chapter will explore the interplay between the mechanics of sex and the emotional side of intimate relationships.

To help frame the issues, here is a point-counterpoint presenting what seem to be opposing positions on this subject:

- True love is a catalyst for great sex.
- Great sex makes true love stronger and better.

- Love is the key to keeping one's sex life alive through the years.
- Great sexual technique is important to keeping love alive over time.

- It's possible for a couple to be in love despite mediocre or non-existent sex.
- It's possible to have terrific sex without being in love.

- Good sex can't cure serious problems a couple might have.
- Bad sex isn't the source of most couple's problems.

As you thought about each pair of statements, it may have struck you that perhaps it's not a case of either-or: all of the statements can be true. Love and sex are constantly interacting within a romantic relationship in ways that can be synergistic.

And yet *techniques*—ways for lovers to have the "great sex" that we see advertised on the covers of women's magazines and countless books and videos—are often disparaged by sexual purists. There are five major lines of attack:

- Sexual techniques can be used to seduce and exploit the innocent.
- Sexual techniques are associated with casual, love-less relationships.
- Sexual techniques make intercourse more complicated than it needs to be.
- Sexual techniques are superficial; sex should express our true inner selves.

• Sexual techniques are artificial; good sex should come naturally.

These are valid concerns, especially in today's sexually obsessed world with so much exploitation all around us. So it's important to explore each of these concerns in some depth.

> **Mutually satisfying lovemaking—where both partners have an orgasm— is learned, not instinctive.**

Techniques Are Used for Seduction and Exploitation

The worst fear of those who trash sexual techniques is that they can be used to seduce the innocent in liaisons that are "casual" for the abuser (usually a sexually experienced man) and traumatic for the victim (usually a naive young woman). There is certainly a long history of this dynamic, but if girls and women have their wits about them and know what to look for, they can easily see through an exploitative seduction attempt.

In the diagram on page 134, the upper left-hand quadrant is where seduction might take place—no love but sexual techniques used skillfully and unscrupulously.

Sophisticated sexual techniques		
No knowledge of sexual techniques		
	Not in love	Deeply in love

The good news is that most cads and sexual exploiters tend to stay in character: they don't give a hoot about their partner's satisfaction (takes too long; too much trouble) and are unlikely to use techniques that bring their seduction target to orgasm. As young women venture into the world of men, this provides a way of spotting sexual exploitation. A red light should start flashing with any sexual technique that tilts more toward his pleasure than hers. The bottom-line question is this: *Do his actions (not just his words) show that he cares about my sexual satisfaction at least as much as he does about his own?* Females who keep this question in mind can immediately tell the difference between an exploitative sexual gambit and the behavior one would look for in a true lover. In addition, girls and women have legal tools that previous generations did not have: our heightened consciousness of sexual harassment, sexual abuse, and rape has raised the stakes for men who might be thinking about playing the old seduction game.

Techniques Enable Casual Sex

A second concern about sexual techniques is that they will lead young people into superficial, loveless relationships. The worry here is that lust has a life of its own. It's always been possible to enjoy sexual pleasure and orgasms quite apart

> **Do sexual techniques interfere with spontaneous lovemaking? Are they necessary when people are really in love?**

from a loving relationship (masturbation, sex with a prostitute, casual sex, etc.). In her 1973 novel *Fear of Flying*, Erica Jong coined the term "zipless fuck" to describe a passionate liaison with no emotional strings attached. Recent accounts of contemporary teenagers "hooking up" sexually (this often means the girl performing oral sex on the boy) indicate that this pattern is very much alive today.

Years after writing her novel, Jong penned a provocative follow-up in which she wondered if we are asking too much of our primary relationships and suggested that the best sex may occur outside of marriage.

The problem with Americans is that unlike the French, we want all our emotional eggs in one basket. We crave passion, sex, friendship, and children all with the same partner. Can such miracles occur? And if they occur, how long can they last...since passion is about fantasy and marriage is about reality, passion and marriage are the oddest of bedfellows. Yes, wild passionate sex exists. It can even exist in marriage. But it is occasional, not daily. And it is not the only thing that keeps people together. Talking and laughing keeps people together. Shared goals keep couples together.

Jong goes on to say that passionate sex is too intense for many people, and this is why they shy away from it:

The busyness of marriage is real, but we also use it to protect us from raw intimacy, from having to be too open too much of the time. Pleasure is terrifying because it breaks down the boundaries between people. Embracing passion means living with fear.

If Jong is right, some couples may actually *prefer* "parallel play"—you do me, I do you, and let's call it a night.

Is the promotion of sexual techniques by sex books and videos adding to the number of superficial, loveless "hook-ups" in our society? Maybe it's the other way around. It seems more plausible that adults and teenagers who want to avoid true intimacy *choose* sexual techniques that distance them from close emotional contact and *avoid* techniques (such as mutual orgasms) that bring them face to face with a lover, eyes wide open, at the peak of sexual and emotional passion. The avoidance of intimacy among many couples is beyond the scope of this book, but it does suggest that sexual techniques, however widely disseminated, may not be the driving force behind the number of "zipless fucks" we're hearing about today.

Techniques Make Sex Too Complicated

Those who disparage sexual techniques say that all this methodology is gimmicky, distracting, and antithetical to the way love should be—and they have a point. With hundreds of variations of foreplay and sexual position, many sex books and videos are not only complicated; they're intimidating. For a couple earnestly pursuing this kind of advice, sex may seem like an Olympic event—a *project!*

The truth is that most of these techniques, while titillating and intriguing, aren't essential to mutual satisfaction. Sexual positions (all of which are variations on five basic ones: missionary, woman on top, side-by-side, standing up, and rear entry) can add variety, but they are not at the heart of good lovemaking. Nor are the toys, gizmos, and other accoutrements of so-called advanced sex. What matters is having a mutually satisfactory way for both partners to have orgasms (not necessarily simultaneous) when they make love. And as we have seen in the two previous chapters, there are few reliable, accessible ways that this can happen—none of them very complicated.

> **Sexual techniques with a small "t"—pointers on foreplay, positions, toys, etc.— can enhance lovemaking but don't address the deeper issue of mutual satisfaction.**

This suggests the need to distinguish between sexual technique with a small "t"—foreplay methods, positions, toys, and devices—and sexual technique with a capital "T"—finding ways to reliably bring both partners to orgasm when they make love. Both kinds are integral to making love, but technique with a capital "T" goes much deeper and is essential to finding mutual satisfaction in a love relationship.

Techniques Don't Allow the Expression of One's True Sexual Self

In their 2001 book, *Sexual Intelligence*, Sheree Conrad and Michael Milburn wrote: "The key to a great sex life is not what we *do* in bed—anyone can learn a new technique—but rather what is going on in our minds, often without our clear awareness, while we are engaged in sexual behavior."

True enough. Struggling to learn and apply a new sexual technique can produce superficial, inauthentic behavior, and there's a plausible argument for allowing our untutored sexual personality to express itself in bed.

But if we do this, *will our partners like what they see?* A lover's actions during sex usually place him or her somewhere on each of the classic "OCEAN" personality dimensions:

> **Techniques with a capital "T"—addressing the perennial challenge of both partners having orgasms—are at the heart of a fulfilling sex life.**

Open to experience <————————> Incurious
Conscientious <————————> Undirected
Extroverted <————————> Introverted
Agreeable <————————> Antagonistic
Neurotic <————————> Stable

A person who is more toward the neurotic or incurious end of the spectrum, for example, may not be a good lover right off the bat.

The question is whether learning a sexual technique

can mask these personality traits (and others that work against good, mutual lovemaking). Maybe, maybe not. It depends on whether a person is willing to listen and learn and change what's not working in bed. But there are limits here. Lovers tend to *choose* sexual techniques (or balk at learning them) based on their personalities and their innate sexual likes and dislikes. This means that if people are being authentic (no play-acting, no techniques), sex is an ideal arena in which to catch a glimpse of a person's true make-up (and to ask whether he or she is a good match). The difficult part is knowing what's authentic and what's not.

To complicate things even more, basic temperament is not the only thing that is revealed during sex. When two people climb into bed, they both carry a lot of baggage from a lifetime of sexual experiences. Many of us still harbor feelings of shame and inhibition from times when parents scolded us about nudity, touching ourselves "down there," and using "filthy words." We also carry our culture's idealized images of "perfect" male and female bodies, which can cause intense self-consciousness during sex (even with the lights out). Many of us have a personal template for sexual arousal and pleasure derived from masturbation and sexual fantasy, and it may or may not be a good fit with our partner's template. Often we carry baggage from previous sexual partners, including emotional bruises, embarrassing moments, and wistful memories that can haunt us with a new lover. And all too many of us have deep wounds from sexual abuse or betrayal—feelings of hurt, humiliation, and shame that can greatly complicate the enjoyment of sex with another person.

Psychologist Donn Byrne believes that based on previous experiences, people tend to fall into two groups: erotophiles and erotophobes:

> **"Great sex" is a way of having mutually satisfying intercourse that is sustainable over time.**

- Erotophiles have been shaped by generally positive experiences with sex, while erotophobes have traveled a bumpier road, sometimes involving sexual abuse.
- Erotophiles believe that sex is an important part of life; erotophobes would like to tuck it away in a corner.
- Erotophiles have no problem talking about sex; erotophobes are uncomfortable using sex words.
- Erotophiles tend to be sexually liberated and move easily into physical relationships; erotophobes are more conservative, but are driven by the same biological urges as everyone else and usually end up having sex despite their inhibitions.

• Erotophiles are comfortable enough to raise concerns about getting pregnant and are likely to use birth control; erotophobes, inhibited about using sex vocabulary, tend to be swept up in the inarticulate passion of the moment and are less likely to use birth control and therefore have a higher rate of unintended pregnancy. (This research was done before HIV/AIDS; if Byrne surveyed people today, he would probably find that erotophobes have a higher rate of sexual infections and HIV/AIDS than erotophiles.)

Byrne's theory suggests that the imprint of early life experiences plays a major role in shaping sexual attitudes and behavior. Do our personal histories and basic temperament create a hardwired sexual personality? If so, we are what we are, and learning a new sexual technique isn't going to have much effect.

So are all those instructional books and videos a waste of time, beyond the titillation? It's certainly naive to think that learning sexual techniques can overcome deep inhibitions and transform people's basic temperaments, turning erotophobes into erotophiles and selfish jerks into great lovers. But people aren't programmed for life. It's possible to come to terms with past experiences and even neutralize the damage done by sexual abuse with skillful counseling and therapy. It's possible for a person to reflect on how certain patterns of behavior are repeatedly causing problems in relationships. People can change. Redemption is possible. With candid feedback from friends and lovers, good communication, thoughtful introspection—and, yes, some work on basic sexual techniques—almost everyone should be able to launch into romance with an open heart.

Ah, romance. This is where things get complicated. How important is sex in love relationships—and what is the interplay between romance and love? Oscar Wilde once wrote: "A man wants to be a woman's first love; a woman wants to be a man's last romance." But Wilde was talking about men wanting to marry virgins and women wanting their husbands to stop sowing wild oats and settle down (sentiments that are still with us).

What do we mean by romance today? In a 1992 study, psychologist Raymond Tucker of Bowling Green State University found that both men and women have a deeply romantic streak—but also a curious ambivalence about the place of sex in relation to love and romance. He asked people, "What constitutes a romantic act?" A rank-ordered list of the responses he received is on the next page.

For Men	For Women
1. Taking walks together	1. Taking walks together
2. Kissing	2. Flowers
3. Candle-lit dinners	3. Kissing
4. Cuddling	4. Cuddling
5. Hugging	5. Candle-lit dinners
6. Flowers	6. Declaring "I love you"
7. Holding hands	7. Love Letters
8. Making love	8. Slow dancing
9. Love letters	9. Hugging
10. Sitting by the fireplace.	10. Giving surprise gifts

It's touching that both men and women have so much in common in their notions of romantic acts. But what's most striking in these responses is that sex is not very prominent on either list; making love ranked eighth among the men and didn't even make the top ten for women. Why this disconnect between intercourse and romance? Do most of these folks have lousy sex lives?

That's possible, considering how many people (especially women) say they are disappointed with sex. But it's also possible that Tucker's subjects thought that his question about romantic acts was not about their sex lives. Sure, sex can be romantic, but what popped into their heads when they were asked about romance was the emotional/feeling side of relationships: love letters, walking on the beach, candlelit dinners, and the like.

This gives us an intriguing glimpse of people's attitudes about romance, sex, and love—and the way they may *not* be interacting in many people's relationships.

Psychologist Robert Sternberg has a theory that takes this idea a little deeper. Sternberg postulates that true love can be seen as a triangle with three components:

Passion—the lovers are physically attracted and have a sexual relationship;

Intimacy—the lovers are best friends and communicate effortlessly;

Commitment—the lovers agree to be faithful to each other.

There are many possible combinations of these three aspects of love, most of which fall short of what Sternberg calls *consummate* love. These include:

- Infatuation (passion only)
- Friendship (intimacy only)
- Empty love (commitment only)
- Romantic love (intimacy and passion)
- Fatuous love (commitment and passion)

• Companionate love (intimacy and commitment)

With consummate or true love, all three sides of the triangle are active in the relationship, and each side interacts with the other two:

- Intimacy and good communication enhance the enjoyment of sex—and deepen the commitment and the desire to stay together.
- Passion (sex) deepens intimacy by expressing affection at another level—and strengthens commitment by holding lovers together through the vicissitudes of life.
- Commitment creates a safe and trusting environment in which people can really let go and enjoy themselves sexually—and constantly creates new history for the couple to share.

In short, there's a powerful synergy among the three sides of the triangle:

- Sex is better with intimacy and commitment.
- Intimacy is deeper with commitment and sex.
- Commitment is stronger with sex and intimacy.

All this helps put sex in context, and suggests a way to think about sexual techniques in a truly loving relationship: necessary but not sufficient. Ideally, techniques are always operating in a way that allows the authentic expression of our inner selves—but we can always learn and grow as people and work at becoming better lovers.

Sexual Techniques Keep Us from Doing What Comes Naturally

Sex in the context of love and romance sometimes takes on an almost mystical quality. The lovers run through the field in slow motion. They stop and turn toward each other in the sunset. Their eyes lock. They kiss. Slow fadeout. *But what happens after the fadeout?* Not to worry, because when people are really in love, they know what to do.

Unfortunately, this is a lie, and the movies and other vehicles of romantic mythology do a great disservice when they continue to propagate it. Yes, sex comes naturally. But when couples go totally by instinct, the sex is rarely great—especially for the woman—and even when the sex is good at first it often does not stand the test of time. Lovemaking that brings genuine satisfaction to both partners over time is neither easy nor obvious. Having sex is innate; mutually satisfying lovemaking is learned.

When the basics of sexual technique (with a capital "T") are not learned, sex can be disappointing and drag down the whole relationship. Using Sternberg's triangle again, this time looking at negative synergy, it's easy to see how problems on the sexual side can affect the other two, souring communication and undermining commitment. According to sex therapist Charles Muir, there's a disproportionate impact when a downward spiral begins: "When sex is good, it's 10 percent of the relationship. When it's bad, it's 90 percent."

Young couples need to learn fundamental sexual techniques. In fact, it's downright unfair to expect every new couple to unravel the challenges that have flummoxed lovers for thousands of years. The confusing asymmetries of men's and women's sexual anatomies, the seductive myth that penetration produces female orgasm, the challenges of pacing and timing—this is a lot to figure out. Strong love with zero sexual technique (the bottom right quadrant on the diagram on page 134) is not the best place for a couple to be. To get into the top right-hand quadrant (true love with sexual proficiency), it really helps to be exposed to some fundamental insights that have been discovered over the years. Technique is certainly not everything, and it can't solve deep incompatibilities, but getting basic information early in a relationship can save a lot of time and resentment and help lovers get to the heart of the matter—lasting sexual happiness—a lot sooner.

> Mutually satisfying sex combines with love to take a romantic relationship to a higher level. That's what sexual happiness is all about.

"Love is all you need/Love is all you need…" sang the Beatles. But love is not enough, and neither is giving flowers, walking on the beach, and snuggling by the fireplace. It's certainly important to be in love and get along and communicate well on a day-to-day basis, and yes, people can survive for a lifetime without great sex. But without some basic knowledge about how to make intercourse mutually satisfying, many couples will spend years figuring things out and may never arrive at truly satisfying lovemaking.

Communication: The Key to Joining Love and Sex

For couples who are having difficulty finding their way to mutually satisfying sex, the most powerful technique is being able to talk openly and honestly about sex. Unfortunately, says sex therapist Judith Seifert, "Most people find it easier to have sex than to talk about it." There's something about expressing preferences in bed—saying what we like and what we don't like— that's very challenging. We want to be pleasing and passionate ("Yes, yes, yes!"), but the words are difficult to find when things are not going well ("Not that way; here, let me show you."). We don't want to come across as demanding and judgmental and hurt the other person's feelings ("Not like that!"), and we certainly don't want to spoil the moment. But people are not mind-readers. All this reticence leads straight to "Not tonight, I'm too tired."

Compare this reticence to a situation where feedback

flows naturally: having someone scratch your back. You have no hesitation saying, "A little bit lower. To the left. A little further over. Right there. Not quite so hard. Yes! A little more. Ahhhhh! OK, that's enough. Thank you!" Why can't we give feedback like this for, say, stimulating the clitoris? That's the only way it's going to be done right, because the woman knows what she's feeling and what's needed to bring her to orgasm. But many women hesitate to give honest and specific feedback, especially at the beginning of a sexual relationship. They're afraid of hurting their partners' feelings, making them feel incompetent, coming across as selfish and pushy, and driving them away.

Sex-advice columnist Amy Spencer shared a telling personal story about not speaking up. Her boyfriend thought that she didn't like to make love in the morning. In fact, she did, but rebuffed his advances because she was turned off by "the halitosis from Hades, the chin grit suitable for sanding pine furniture, the way he slept with his black dress socks on." If he had known all this, he probably would have addressed her grievances immediately, but she could never bring herself to tell him, and he never thought to ask.

Here we have the classic hesitation waltz of poor sexual communication. She can't bring herself to speak up. She hopes that he will figure it out, but he doesn't. He assumes that she will tell him if there's a problem, but she doesn't. Perhaps unconsciously, she's putting him through a mind-reading test, and the poor guy flunks. The problem festers under the surface, producing resentment and frustration. In this case (as in many others), lack of communication kills the relationship.

If a man can't ask in a nice way what the problem is with sex in the morning, and if his lover can't ask him to do something as simple as brush his teeth, shave, and take off those damn socks, how much more difficult is it going to be for them to talk about some truly intimate sexual concerns—for example, touching her clitoris a little differently? But this is the state of communication between many, many lovers. Given the deep roots of our sexual reticence, it's really hard to talk openly.

One short-term solution for couples who are having difficulty putting their thoughts into words is to use an indirect approach to sharing sexual likes and dislikes. In *The Good Orgasm Guide*, British sexologist Kate Taylor has these suggestions:

- Respond audibly (not necessarily with words) to things that your lover does that are pleasurable and fun; this provides encouragement for him or her to continue. (In the case of the spurned morning lover, this might consist of complimenting him on his freshly shaved face, sweet-smelling breath, and lovely naked feet when they make love in the early evening. Hint, hint.)

- Extinguish things your lover does that are not working for you by not responding. (Of course if something is painful, uncomfortable, or degrading, you need to speak up.)
- In asking your lover what he or she likes, give either/or choices the way your eye doctor does when zeroing in on the correct prescription for a new pair of glasses: Which do you like better, this way (demonstrate), or this way (demonstrate)? It's a lot easier to express a preference between two options than to ask for something directly.
- If you're having difficulty pleasing your partner, ask him or her to take you by the hand and show you nonverbally.

These are starting points. They can help get the flow of honest feedback going between lovers, and can serve as bridges to the ultimate goal—being able to come right out and say it. The key is listening to feedback, communicating honestly, and keeping your eyes on the prize: genuine, mutual satisfaction for both partners by the end of each lovemaking session.

Does sex make love better? Does love make sex better? *Yes*! What's technique got to do with it? *Plenty*. Being in love is where it all begins, and the interaction of all three sides of love—intimacy, commitment, and sexual passion—is what fuels a deep and lasting love relationship. But if a couple does not have a good approach to making love with mutual satisfaction (i.e., both having orgasms), their love will not reach its full potential. And if they are stuck with a technique that consistently frustrates one partner, their love (no matter how deep) will suffer. Orgasms matter. It's hardwired.

The point needs to be made once again: making love in a way that deeply pleases both partners is not easy or obvious; it doesn't come naturally to the vast majority of people. Learning sexual techniques with a capital "T" helps people cut to the chase earlier in their relationships. There's a lot more to long-term happiness than good sex, but basic sexual technique is deeply entwined with lasting love.

Chapter Eight

Keeping Passion Alive in Long-Term Relationships

As lovers segue from the hotly passionate courtship stage into a more companionate long-term relationship, it's only natural for them to worry about their sex lives—with thoughts like: there used to be a lot of fireworks, but now sex is getting boring; we used to make love practically every day, but now we're so busy that it's happening less often; sex used to last for hours, but with the kids around, we can't find the time—and quite often we're just not in the mood. Couples who are no longer hitting youthful performance targets for sexual variety, frequency, duration, and spontaneity may fret that the magic is gone and their love affair is on the slippery slope to doom.

> **Couples who no longer have as much sexual variety, frequency, duration, and spontaneity as they did when they were younger may worry that the magic in their relationship is gone.**

This could be true, for any number of reasons. But the problem might also be that the couple has unrealistic expectations about sex—that it must be different every time, happen every single day, last for hours, and always be triggered by spontaneous passion. This chapter points toward a more realistic set of expectations in each of these areas, and also to the critical importance of having a viable route to mutual satisfaction—one that is comfortable and acceptable for both partners, is easy to use, and keeps working over the years.

The Issue of Boredom

Why do some couples get bored with sex after a few months while others continue to enjoy making love throughout their adult lives? The conventional wisdom is that the way to stave off sexual boredom is *variety*—that "great sex" consists of different positions, different techniques, different routines, different times of day, different venues, different toys and devices, different perfumes, different condom colors—and different lovers. Much of contemporary sex material caters to this view, constantly feeding people new ideas on how to add to the sexual menu. Why else would all those women's magazines tout a sex article on the cover of every single issue?

Variety-oriented sex advice focuses almost exclusively on foreplay. That's understandable, since there are endless permutations to the positions and possibilities of this part of lovemaking. The whole body is an erogenous zone, and if a couple has the time, the imagination, and the stamina, foreplay can be new and interesting practically forever. Most sex advice spends little if any time on the way in which couples have their orgasms—because, as we saw in earlier chapters, there are relatively few effective approaches to this part of lovemaking.

> **Many people assume that variety is the way to avoid sexual boredom: different positions, different techniques, different venues, different toys, different condom colors—and different lovers.**

But is variety during foreplay really the key to avoiding sexual boredom? Two people can make love in an outrageous number of ways and still grow weary of each other sexually. This can happen if they've fallen out of love, been betrayed, or suffer from other problems, but it can also happen to couples who are in love and really want to make the relationship work. Could it be that another variable is more important to the staying power of a sexual relationship?

This is an empirical question; we could find the answer by doing really thorough, honest, confidential interviews with couples for whom lovemaking has and hasn't stood the test of time. Unfortunately, sex literature is not particularly helpful in this important area—probably because researchers haven't been asking the right questions. More about that in Chapter 9.

While we wait for better research, though, we can speculate about what truly keeps passion alive. Here's a theory; it's unproven, but it poses an intriguing alternative to the idea that variety is everything.

In the early stages of a romantic relationship lovers are full of passion and excitement and often experiment with lots of different positions and approaches and explore their likes and dislikes. As they get to know each other better they tend to settle into a routine—certain preliminaries and a specific way of reaching (or not reaching) orgasms—with occasional variations. This is a crucial point in a sexual relationship. Are both partners having satisfying orgasms (not necessarily simultaneous) when they make love? If a couple's routine leaves one partner sexually unsatisfied (and it's almost always the woman), there is trouble ahead. These lovers may confide in their friends that sex has become "boring," but boredom is not the real issue. The nub of the matter is a lack of deep satisfaction for the woman, which robs lovemaking of mutuality and depth—and may affect her partner's level of satisfaction as well; men may be more sensitive to the subtle dynamics of sex than we suppose.

Without the deep satisfaction of mutual orgasms,

there's a tendency to focus on sexual behaviors that by themselves can seem repetitive and even tiresome. It *is* boring to go through the same routine week after week if it doesn't culminate in good mutual orgasms. The hypothesis here is that if we interviewed couples who have become "bored" with sex and asked the right questions, we would find that they do not have a good technique for mutual orgasms. We would predict that such couples would become increasingly dissatisfied with their sex life and either accept that (and have a sexless marriage), use other means to gain satisfaction (perhaps masturbation), or look for new partners to try to recreate the "sheer excitement" phase that they remember so fondly.

Conversely, if we interviewed couples who have been genuinely happy with their sex life for several years,

> **What truly quenches our sexual appetite and leaves a sense of deep gratification and closeness is not all the foreplay; it's the *orgasms*.**

our prediction would be that at some point they discovered a good sexual finale and continued to use it (perhaps with variations) over time.

But doesn't using the same mutual-orgasm approach get monotonous? Strangely enough, it doesn't. People don't get tired of having orgasms together any more than they get tired of eating good food. The analogy with food works on a number of levels.

- Our appetite for food and for sex are basic drives that build up over time. When we've had a fine meal or a good orgasm, we feel mellow and satisfied and our drives are temporarily slaked.
- Both types of hunger are influenced by quality: when food or lovemaking is mediocre, our appetite goes down; when the meal or the sex is good, our appetite increases.
- If we're extremely hungry or haven't had sex in a long time, we are less fussy about the finer points of cuisine and lovemaking.
- With both food and sex, we can have too much of a good thing: with food we feel sick to our stomachs; with sex, we get exhausted and sore. In both cases, our appetite disappears, and we have no desire to eat or make love for a period of time. But the basic drives are still there, and before long, they're back.

But the food/sex analogy breaks down in one area. Although we can get great enjoyment in the course of eating and making love, what truly quenches our sexual appetite and leaves a sense of deep gratification and closeness is not all the foreplay; it's the *orgasms*. The kissing, hugging, different positions, techniques, toys, etc., can be great fun, sharpen the palate and heighten sexual arousal, and even boost the eventual level of gratification—but unlike the courses of a good meal (which *are* the meal), foreplay activities are *a means to an end*; it's the orgasmic finale that really hits the spot. The quality of this final stage of lovemaking is what delivers the lasting physical and emotional payoff. Getting that part right is the key—a point that sex books and videos rarely emphasize.

Another reason that using the same mutual-orgasm technique can be satisfying year after year is that the feelings lovers experience from orgasms can change from session to session. One of the remarkable things about sex is the potential for great variety within the same technique. Lovemaking in which a couple uses a single mutual-orgasm approach can be hot and lustful, sweet and gentle, loud and raunchy, whispery and quiet, and everything in between. Subtle differences in mood, time of month, level of arousal, positions, pressure, and timing can produce quite different feelings and climaxes. So within the context of one successful approach to mutual orgasms, there can be great variety over the years.

> **A couple might make love every day on a romantic vacation, but the expectation that sex needs to happen on a daily basis month after month is a killer. People need to recharge their batteries!**

How do lovers know if they have found a good mutual-orgasm technique? There are several ways to tell:

- First, does it deliver a satisfying climax to both partners during a lovemaking session?
- Second, is it acceptable and comfortable for both partners?
- Third, does it still work on a Friday night when both partners are pretty weary? (Let's face it: most couples with children have limited options for private lovemaking time, most of which are times when they're not fresh and well-rested.)
- Finally, does it continue to work for both partners over the years?

These questions may be the best indicators available to loving couples as their relationship moves through the years. If they are honest with each other, they will know the answer to the first and second questions quite early on. They'll get the answer to the third question as life gets busier and they're more exhausted on weekends, and the answer to the fourth will become apparent after a few years. If they're always "too tired" for sex on Friday night and sex is becoming "boring," it's a sure sign that the couple needs to go back to questions one and two and find a different route to mutual orgasms that really works for both of them.

The bottom line: Sexual boredom can happen—but it doesn't have to. People can get bored with specific foreplay techniques, but they never get tired of having orgasms. Novelty can be an aphrodisiac in the short run, but it's not a good long-term strategy. Sexual wisdom lies in getting into a groove with a good sexual finale technique. Couples who do this aren't in a rut; they're on a roll.

The Issue of Frequency

After the intensely romantic opening months of a relationship, how often lovemaking takes place can become a troublesome issue. In the film *Annie Hall*, there's a scene in which Alvie Singer (played by Woody Allen) and his lover, Annie Hall (Diane Keaton), are shown in split-screen talking to their therapists:

> His psychiatrist: "How often do you sleep together?"
> Alvie: "Hardly ever, maybe three times a week."
> Her psychiatrist: "Do you have sex often?"
> Annie: "Constantly, I'd say three times a week."

This scene is funny because it plays on the stereotype of men being sexually insatiable and women shying away from sex. But if Alvie and Annie were a real couple and we were their therapists, we might find that her wish to have intercourse less often stems from her impatience and frustration at not getting any real satisfaction with her klutzy lover, and we might find that his desire for more sex is because, yes, he's a horny guy, but also because he is picking up on her unhappiness and naively thinks that more sex will make it better.

It may also be that Alvie likes multiple orgasms and Annie doesn't. There's a lot of individual variation in this area: for about 90 percent of couples, one intense orgasm is all they need and they're off to dreamland. For others, several orgasms are possible, with a time-out between each inning. And some women are able to have multiple rapid-fire orgasms within the same at-bat. These innate differences can cause sexual incompatibility if a man and woman are at opposite ends of the spectrum. Some couples are successful at talking through or working around such differences. Other couples may reluctantly conclude that they are just not sexually compatible.

> "Routine" sex on weekends doesn't have to be a perfunctory quickie. With a good mutual-orgasm technique, it can be deeply fulfilling virtually every time.

But most lovers (90 percent, if surveys are to be believed) are in the same ballpark in terms of their level of sexual athleticism, so the statistical odds of compatibility on this dimension are high. For the vast majority of lovers, the key is the *quality*, not the quantity, of their lovemaking—and here, once again, the most important thing is having an approach to mutual orgasms that works for both partners. Most couples settle into a routine of having intercourse one to three times per week. If the couple's orgasm technique is working well, this may be enough to satisfy both partners' latent lust. If a couple doesn't have a good technique, frequency may loom large in their minds (as it did, perhaps, for Alvie and Annie)—but frequency is not the real problem.

The one-to-three times a week average puts sex into perspective: a man and woman who make love with that frequency (assuming about 30 minutes per session) are spending six-tenths of one percent of their total time on sex, which means they are spending 99.4 percent of their lives doing other things. This may not seem like very much time for sex (young lovers are at it a lot more than that!), but for married people with full lives, or for older couples whose bodies are slowing down a little, it may be just about enough to satisfy their biological and emotional needs—provided they have satisfying mutual orgasms. In fact, having a lot more sex than this can take the edge off enjoyment. A couple might make love every day on a romantic vacation, but the expectation that sex should happen on a daily basis every single week, month after month is a killer. No matter how good the orgasm technique is, this will make sex into a chore. Many people find that orgasms are more powerful after a few days of abstinence; built-up libido makes lovemaking that much more satisfying when it occurs.

What about times when sex is impossible? Any number of reasons can conspire to keep a couple from making love as frequently as they would like: exhaustion, illness, menstruation, urinary-tract infections, the final stages of pregnancy, a new baby, children waking up with nightmares, ups and downs in the relationship, worries at work, travel, and other intrusions on the routine. It's at times like these that there is the greatest temptation to stray. But the emotional and health risks of infidelity are enormous, as many have learned to their sorrow. Temporary abstinence or masturbation look far better when a couple is in a sexless dry spell.

The Issue of Duration

When newly infatuated lovers engage in sexual "outer-course" (touching but no penetration), sex can last all night. This may be because both are full of fresh passion, find the novelty of a new partner highly arousing, or haven't yet worked out an approach that brings about mutual orgasms and sends them into dreamland. When couples graduate to intercourse, the amount of lovemaking time usually decreases, and as people become better acquainted with each other's sexual responses, sex becomes more "efficient," to the point where it can take less than half an hour.

This can be good and bad: it's good if a couple can have satisfying sex despite being tuckered out or not having much private time; it's bad if those sessions are perfunctory, loveless, and ungratifying. So the issue is not the quantity of time but the quality of lovemaking. We tend to assume that the less time a session lasts, the less enjoyment there is, and there's something to that: longer foreplay (within reason) extends the pleasure and enhances the quality of orgasms, and people's most memorable bouts of lovemaking tend to be extended trysts in idyllic vacation spots with absolutely no time pressure. But sex on normal weekends (or times that can be captured during the week) doesn't have to be a perfunctory quickie. Once again, the key is having a good technique for mutual orgasms. For couples who have found one, even a brief roll in the hay can be deeply satisfying for both partners.

Married couples whose children sleep in nearby bedrooms have another challenge—keeping the sexual noise level down. Back when they were teenagers, most people felt the need to be fairly hush-hush about masturbation.

> **Couples who make love only when both are "in the mood" may find themselves waiting for a long time. Better to get the ball rolling and get themselves in the mood.**

The same was probably true when they were young lovers conducting early, furtive liaisons within earshot of parents, siblings, or college roommates. But when they found more private spots, their lovemaking became more vocal and expressive.

The noises people make during sex are intensely personal (another reason for suppressing them); as trust grows between lovers, inhibitions fade and expressions of pleasure and ecstasy tend to become an important way of expressing love. But when children overhear their parents' sexual noises, they are often confused ("Daddy, why are you hurting Mommy?"). As a result, most couples with children stifle their full-throated expressions of enjoyment for a number of years—and appreciate those occasions when they have the apartment or house to themselves or are ensconced in a hotel room with good thick walls.

A final worry couples have about duration is that sex will literally shrivel up when they are in their sixties and seventies—the age-old afflictions of vaginal dryness and erectile dysfunction. Isn't it ironic that early in our sex lives, the opposite is true: young women have a surfeit of vaginal lubrication (often leaving a wet spot in bed) and young men have too darn many erections (sometimes at embarrassing moments) and tend to ejaculate too quickly during intercourse.

The good news for aging lovers is that there's now a much greater comfort level talking about these formerly taboo subjects; we have a better handle on the factors affecting sexual health (smoking, exercise, and obesity, among others); and there are effective medications for erection problems (Viagra and others) and excellent vaginal lubricants. The best news is that our sex organs continue to function throughout life: men can continue to have orgasms into their eighties and nineties, and women have been assured by Natalie Angier that "your clitoris will always be there for you." Most couples who stay healthy, use the available remedies, and keep the lines of communication open can continue to have a robust sex life right through their senior years.

Being in the Mood

In the passionate opening months of a romantic relationship, lovers are interested in having sex pretty much any time, and spontaneity is the name of the game. A wink, a raised eyebrow, or a secret phrase is all that's needed for them to tumble into bed. But as couples get more immersed in work, kids, hobbies, community, etc., there's less free-floating libido, and the times when each partner is in the mood for sex become less frequent—and are less often in synch.

The factors that influence being in the mood are many and varied. A romantic candlelit dinner can make two hearts go pitter-pat. Erotic movies, music, books, and works of art often get the juices flowing. An enforced period of abstinence can turn the temperature up. Some women are more lustful at certain points in their menstrual cycle. And there are times when lustful thoughts arise for no apparent reason. The problem is that for busy people, these sexualized moments don't always occur at the most opportune times, and the moments when *both* partners are in the mood within the same one-hour period may be few and far between.

But this doesn't mean that a couple's sex life has to be put on hold until those rare occasions when both sets of loins are stirring simultaneously. In fact, the belief that both partners must be spontaneously in the mood for sex to happen can cause major problems in a relationship. A couple can wait for *weeks* for the planets to align; during that time, one partner may make several sexual overtures and have the unpleasant and deflating experience of being rebuffed ("Not tonight…"). This can lead the spurned partner to retaliate in kind when the now-eager partner finally proposes sex ("Sorry, but my back is killing me."). A dynamic like this can create strong resentment and ripple into other parts of the relationship.

The problem here is the underlying assumption that the only good sex is spontaneous sex. It's simply not true. Just because sex isn't happening at the drop of a hat doesn't mean that the magic in the relationship is gone. In the words of Michele Weiner Davis in *The Sex-Starved Marriage*, "waiting for the urge to strike is pointless; better to bash ahead and hope for the best."

The euphemism "in the mood" may also be part of the problem. When we say we are in the mood, we mean that we are mildly (or highly) aroused. But if we say we are not in the mood, it sounds like our mental state can't be changed for a while (until we *are* in the mood)—whereas if we say that we are not aroused right now, there's the possibility that we are *arousable*. One of the great things about human sexuality is that, with the right stimuli (mental or physical), most people can go from zero (thinking of other things with no libido in sight) to 60 (aroused and hot to trot) in a matter of minutes.

But when, oh when, can that happen in the over-scheduled, stressed-out life of a busy couple? Natalie Angier reports on a sophisticated statistical study that sheds some light on this question:

> If you plot the incidence of intercourse among couples, you'll see an amazing statistical high point, and it's called the weekend—not because people necessarily feel sexy each Sunday, but because people have sex when it's convenient, when they're not exhausted by work, and when they have the whole day to toy with. A hormone may lead you to water, but it can't make you drink.

However, the advice to forge ahead and *just do it* is not enough. When people are not spontaneously in the mood, what will motivate them to go about getting themselves aroused? The key is knowing that there is a real sexual payoff for both partners at the other end of making love—and that means having a technique that virtually guarantees real physical and psychological satisfaction. If lovers have one and know that they will almost certainly wind up having good orgasms together, they are more likely to get the ball rolling, even if they are tired and preoccupied. Conversely, if one or both partners are unhappy with their lovemaking technique—if there usually isn't an orgasmic payoff for at least one lover—then sex will seem like too much trouble and there will always be reasons for one or both partners to call it a night. Good sex involves giving pleasure, to be sure, but it's also about getting satisfaction, and if that's not happening, sex inexorably fades over the years.

The hypothesis that was advanced in Chapter 1 was that the absence of good mutual orgasms (rather than exhaustion or job stress or male-female power struggles) is the root cause of a lot of marital abstinence. Here's the reverse of that hypothesis: a really *satisfying* sex life can be part of a positive feedback loop that smoothes out the daily tensions of life and reduces stress from other sources. If this is true, good sex will make a man be more likely to remember to put the toilet seat down and pick up his socks. And helpfulness around the house could in turn result in less resentment about everyday omissions and grease the skids for more and better sex. It's been said that there's nothing sexier these days than a man who takes out the trash without being asked. It seems plausible that this kind of good will between partners can contribute measurably to a willingness to go ahead and get themselves "in the mood."

Fine. But at a very practical level, how and when is the process of getting "in the mood" going to happen? Some busy couples have found that the best strategy is having a tacit agreement that certain times of the week are set aside for making love—times when they are least likely to be interrupted, have a fair amount of stored-up libido, and don't have to worry about an alarm clock waking them up six hours later (sounds a lot like Friday and Saturday night and Sunday morning). At the appointed hour they get the ball rolling—with kissing being the leading favorite because, as Emma Taylor and Lorelei Sharkey so nicely put it, "the kiss is the most compact, powerful, diverse, complex, practically perfect sexual act ever invented." One thing leads to another, and with any luck, they both get in the mood and… (fadeout).

Returning to the gustatory analogy, we may not be actively hungry when we walk into the restaurant, but it's dinner time, our stomachs are empty, and when we smell the food cooking (or feel our tongues intertwining), our appetite is suddenly back. For healthy people who have not had an orgasm all week, sexual urges that seemed to be deeply submerged can come to the surface quite quickly.

People who have default times for lovemaking every week are not forcing themselves to do something they don't want to do; they're just taking steps to ease them-selves out of a predictably asexual mood and do something they really want to do but wouldn't do if they waited for a spontaneous urge to arise. Thanks to their ever-present libido, most people are arous-able pretty much any time—but because of their busy lives and many preoc-cupations, they need a little push to get going.

> **Having regular times for lovemaking and using a good mutual-orgasm technique, with occasional spontaneous variations, can result in deeply satisfying sex that stands the test of time.**

Making intercourse a regular routine doesn't mean that it has be *routine*. Couples who find an approach that consistently gives deep mutual gratification don't get tired of sex, and they almost always make it a cher-ished part of each week (or month) no matter how busy or tired they are (and actively look forward to those times in the parts of their lives that really are routine). They may not be very passionate when they get into bed, and they may not have the time, the energy, or the privacy for an extended session with the full a la carte menu of foreplay. But if they know that in all likelihood they will both have deeply satisfying orgasms together, they are likely to initiate sex and will end up being glad they did. They're not making love because they *need* to; they're doing it because they love each other, know it will end well, and deeply *want* to. Occasional variations in the routine (making love in the morning during a blizzard, or after lunch on a lazy summer's day, or at some other zany time when the spirit moves) add variety and spice to the mix, but the ending is the same—a glow of mutual satisfaction and deepened feelings of intimacy and commitment.

So it's not necessary to wait around for the right mood to strike both partners at the same time—the right time of month, the moonlight, the stars aligned, that certain sparkle in her eyes. By establishing regular sexual times, having a sure-fire route to mutual satisfaction, continuing to experiment with variations, and always being honest and open about what they're feeling, lovers can keep romance cruising through the years, turning that "eighteen-mile rut" into a freeway of love (thank you, Aretha Franklin).

Chapter Nine

Finding Our Way to Sexual Happiness

Chapter 6 described three ways to make love with mutual satisfaction. Chapter 7 argued that sexual techniques with a capital "T" are an integral part of successful love relationships. And Chapter 8 made the case for the importance of effective techniques to keeping passion alive in long-term love relationships. If all this is true, it would certainly appear that today's lovers, in contrast to those who lived in the sexual dark ages described in the earlier chapters, have an open road before them as their sexual relationships develop.

Unfortunately, it's not that simple. Our society still has significant obstacles to balanced and reciprocal lovemaking, among them: disempowered women; poor communication; men not getting it; hang-ups about masturbation; resistance to "outercourse"; a glut of sexual information; and incomplete sex research. Let's look at each of these challenges—and the ways couples might work to overcome them.

1. *Disempowered women.* The reason for a great deal of sexual unhappiness is that men tend to be dominant (and sometimes domineering) in romantic relationships, which means that women are often dependent and needy. Too often women don't feel confident and sure-footed when faced with the dual challenge of setting sexual limits with their partners and being assertive about their own sexual desires. The gains that Western women have made in the economic and political realms—as well as the much greater seriousness with which law enforcement and school officials now treat charges of sexual misconduct—can be the foundation for greater sexual candor, equality, and happiness. Progress is made whenever girls and women are on an a level playing field with their romantic and sexual partners and use their increased power to assert their right to an equal share of sexual satisfaction. In the past, this would have been unthinkable; now it should be within any woman's grasp.

2. *Poor communication.* Three factors combine to keep most people tongue-tied when it comes to talking about sex: most of us are brought up in ways that make us shy and uncomfortable about sex; most lovers know that their partners' sexual self-concepts are fragile, so they tread lightly when it comes to sharing any thoughts that might be seen as negative; and

there are all kinds of myths about what is supposed to happen in bed, leading many to fear that if they don't conform to those expectations, they're not normal. All this leads people to keep their mouths shut when it comes to sharing truly intimate sexual feelings. When lovers don't communicate honestly and openly in bed, it's very difficult to overcome the built-in "geography" challenges when making love.

This is a pity, because sex improves dramatically when both partners— especially the woman— speak up candidly and specifically about sexual likes and dislikes *right at the beginning of an intimate relationship*. There are no absolutes in bed;

> **Perhaps the location of the clitoris isn't a problem after all. It allows sensitive, thoughtful lovers to attain mutual satisfaction virtually every time they make love.**

what's fun for one person may be too raunchy for another; what's arousing for one may seem degrading for the other; what feels like good robust sex for one may be too rough for the other. Sex gets better when both partners are comfortable talking about it, *listen* to each other, and use feedback to become a sensitive and skillful lover for the person they are with. Sex is better when both lovers are *honest* about what they prefer sexually, and at the same time don't limit themselves to what has given them pleasure in the past—when they can say what they don't like and still be open to new approaches. Sex is better when lovers explore and experiment across the full range of (safe) approaches and techniques, find those that work best for them, and remain open to spontaneous departures and new approaches over time. None of this can happen unless lovers communicate well, and that will happen only when parents and school sex education programs do a better job helping young people develop a basic comfort level talking about sex. That comes from practice—talking openly and matter-of-factly about the whole subject.

3. *Men not getting it.* Unfortunately, a good many twenty-first-century men are continuing the eons-old tradition of selfish, inconsiderate, one-sided lovemaking. All too often, their cluelessness is aided and abetted by women who don't speak up in bed—but let's not make excuses for men. Information is readily available on the true source of female sexual satisfaction—and the fact that penetration almost never produces a female orgasm. These insights can be the beginning of an ongoing sexual conversation between lovers. The burden should not be on women to do all the asking, explaining, teaching, limit-setting, and faking. To be sure, there are other issues that need to be addressed—the whole Mars-Venus chasm, men's

difficulty talking about their feelings and taking the plunge into truly intimate relationships, and their perennial problems with commitment. But these deeper issues should no longer be played out against a backdrop of clueless, one-sided sex.

4. *Hang-ups about masturbation.* Our society's continuing nervousness and negativism on the subject of self-pleasuring doesn't make things easier for teenagers—or for adults. We are asking a great deal of adolescents when we lecture them to avoid risky sexual behaviors as they traverse the dangerous waters between the emergence of their sexual appetites (around twelve to thirteen years old) and the age when intercourse is considered appropriate (Late teens? College? Early twenties? Marriage?). Kids almost never hear the important message that masturbation is a safe, healthy sexual outlet during adolescence—and at other times in life when two-person sex is not an option. Masturbation is also excellent preparation for mutual enjoyment down the road—especially for young women, for whom orgasms are not going to happen automatically during intercourse the way they do for men. In most relationships, a woman will need to give her partner some quite specific guidance if she is to have *any* chance of true satisfaction during lovemaking. It will be difficult for her to show him the way unless she has experienced

orgasms on her own and unless both partners have developed an accepting, matter-of-fact attitude toward masturbation (hey, almost everyone does it; what's the problem?).

The problem is that parents find it almost impossible to talk to their kids about masturbation and most sex-education programs in schools and virtually all articles and books about teenage sexuality are extraordinarily gun-shy on the subject. The forced resignation of Surgeon General Jocelyn Elders in 1994 for suggesting that masturbation should be treated more forthrightly in schools was a huge setback (and not a shining moment for her boss, Bill Clinton, who probably should have been doing a little more masturbating himself). Many people seemed to be unable to grasp the difference between teaching *about* masturbation and giving masturbation *lessons*.

Some religious teaching still clings to prohibitions against masturbation, and some of the old myths are still with us in the form of teasing and off-color humor: it causes pimples and warts, it makes hairs grow on your palms, it will make you go blind, and it will turn you into a werewolf! The subtext of a lot of this is that masturbation is for losers—a message that has confused and messed up countless people over the years.

Where will teenagers hear a more positive message?

Must every new generation deal with uncertainty and even shame when succumbing to almost unstoppable natural urges? What would it take for us to *normalize* masturbation and take it off the shame map? Well,

> **The location of the clitoris gives women a way to see through the sweet talk and find out how generous and considerate their partner really is.**

it would be helpful if young people heard the following messages from their elders: masturbation is by far the safest way to release the sexual energy that naturally bubbles up in every healthy person; masturbation is an intensely private and personal choice; and no one should feel ashamed to masturbate (or feel ashamed if they don't).

5. *Resistance to "outercourse."* The risk of pregnancy, HIV/AIDS, and other sexual infections means that any kind of sexual penetration (vaginal, oral, and anal), even with condoms, is risky for couples who don't know and really trust each other. Mutual fondling without penetration ("On me, not in me.") is less complicated, more tilted toward female pleasure, and safer (as long as semen is not ejaculated near the vulva). But some of the hard-core abstinence messages being given to teenagers these days proscribe *any* sexual contact. This is foolish. Young people have

powerful sexual urges starting at puberty, and total suppression of sexual activity for eight to ten years is neither sensible nor realistic.

Dealing with sex and love during this long in-between period is a central challenge of adolescence, and kids need more realistic and supportive advice than they're getting now. There is a lot to be said for abstinence during the teen years—but abstinence should be defined in a way that says safe outercourse is okay (and masturbation, too). In the early stages of a love relationship, outercourse can help lovers (especially teenagers) safely explore their sexuality, learn how each others' bodies work, and prepare for more mutually satisfying intercourse down the road. The only cautionary note is that couples who engage in outercourse need to have the maturity and self-control to resist the strong urge to pass "go" and proceed to penetration. The perennial scenario has been that the male wants increasingly intimate sex and the female has all the responsibility for saying no. In more power-equal relationships, lovers might move beyond this tiresome dynamic, agree in advance on their sexual limits (first base? second base? third base? no penetration), and then have lots of intimate fun within them.

6. *A glut of sexual information and incomplete sex research.* There's tons of information about sex out there—a mind-boggling array of not-very-helpful

advice, enthusiastic endorsements for the one best technique, academic tomes, lectures, TV shows, sex therapists, erotica, and pornography. But virtually all of this material avoids a truly honest examination of the sexual asymmetries between men and women; steers couples up one blind alley after another by suggesting that variety, bizarre practices, a bigger penis, toys, and other paraphernalia are the way to attain sexual bliss; and gives lovers very little guidance finding a mutual orgasm technique that works for them. Who has the time to wade through all this material and separate the thimble full of wheat from the truckloads of chaff? And how many couples have the sexual comfort level and the fabulous communication skills to solve the built-in geography problems on their own? There is a crying need for literature and research that is more helpful to couples as they try to cut to the chase in all the sex information around them and grapple with the very real challenges they face in bed.

A Consumer Guide to Mutual Satisfaction

Taken together, these six barriers are a veritable *moat* between lovers and the enchanted castle of sexual happiness. It's really difficult to level the male-female power balance, improve people's comfort level talking about sex, help men overcome their cluelessness, liberalize attitudes about masturbation and "outercourse," and improve sex research and advice literature. A couple might be able to make progress on the first five—but good, impartial information about sex is something that has to come from the outside.

A worthwhile goal in the years ahead might be a *Consumer Reports*-type guide to making love. If such a guide made use of improved research and critically analyzed all the sexual approaches that have been discovered over the years, it could empower women, serve as a conversation-starter for sexually tongue-tied partners, help men *get it*, and put our society's hangups about masturbation and "outercourse" in perspective.

What would it take to produce this kind of lovemaking guide? First, we would need to get better information on successful and unsuccessful sexual practices by asking couples a few pointed questions about how they have dealt with their bodies' sexual asymmetries. It's interesting that Alfred Kinsey's famous questionnaire had 347 questions and never once used the word "clitoris." Shere Hite's questionnaire asked the right questions, but buried them in scores of others, obscuring her breakthrough findings in a mass of detail. So brevity and focus are key considerations. With any questionnaire, there would also have to be an ironclad guarantee of confidentiality to raise the chances that people would tell the whole truth. Answering questions online seems to be the best way to raise the odds.

Here are ideas for a questionnaire that could generate the data needed to draw more authoritative conclusions about what works and doesn't work over time:

> **Couples are flooded with huge amounts of sex advice, erotica, and pornography, most of it profoundly unhelpful to finding a good technique for having mutual orgasms.**

Questions for women only:

Do you have an orgasm when you make love?

If so, *when* does it happen: before penetration, while your partner's penis is in your vagina, or after he withdraws?

If you do have an orgasm during any part of lovemaking (before, during, or after penetration), *how* do you reach orgasm?

Is this your ideal technique for having an orgasm during lovemaking? If not, what is?

Questions for men only:

At what point during lovemaking does your partner reach orgasm (if at all): before penetration, while your penis is in her vagina, or after you withdraw?

If your partner reaches orgasm during any part of

lovemaking, what specifically brings it about?

Is this your ideal technique? If not, what is?

Questions for both men and women:

How happy or unhappy (sexually) are you with your partner now?

To what do you attribute your level of happiness or unhappiness?

How would you describe your level of sexual satisfaction after making love?

Your partner's?

In roughly what percent of lovemaking sessions do both you and your partner have an orgasm (or more than one orgasm) at some point during the session?

Have you ever faked an orgasm? If so, what made this seem necessary?

If you use a particular technique to reach orgasm, how long have you been using it?

How did you and your partner discover this technique?

Is it effective, comfortable, and acceptable for both you and your partner?

Do both you and your partner find it easy to use?

Has it stood the test of time (i.e., continued to be mutually satisfying for five or more years)?

Have you used other techniques for reaching mutual orgasms? For how long?

How often do you make love? Which days of the

week and what time of day?

How long does an average lovemaking session last?

How do you and your partner decide when to initiate sex?

Have you and your partner ever discussed a sexual problem or concern and resolved it?

If not, what do you feel are the barriers to good communication about sex?

Have you ever felt bored with your sex life? If so, what made you feel this way?

What is the role of masturbation in your life now? What was it in earlier years?

Do you, in all candor, prefer masturbation to intercourse? Why or why not?

If you could be granted any wish, what would you change in your sex life?

Drawing on answers to these questions, the authors of a consumer guide on lovemaking could critically analyze *all* sexual practices and evaluate each mutual-orgasm technique based on four criteria:

- Does it give an orgasm to the man *and the woman* during lovemaking?
- Is it fairly easy to use?
- Is it pleasing and comfortable for both partners?
- Does it stand the test of time?

An authoritative consumer guide to lovemaking based on questions like these is years away, but it's possible to rough out a very preliminary draft from the fragmentary and anecdotal evidence that's available now. Based on the four criteria, the basic approaches to intercourse that are available today could be grouped into three categories:

1. Unacceptable—the woman does not have an orgasm:
   - Wham, bam, thank you, ma'am
   - The woman fakes her orgasms
2. *Caveat emptor*—these "no-hands" techniques are effective for some couples but challenging for many others:
   - Clitoral-hood technique
   - Clitoral bumping technique
   - Coital Alignment Technique (CAT)
   - Hayden technique (the tip of the penis stimulating the clitoris)
   - Riskins' triggering techniques
   - Clitoral stimulation using sexual attachments
3. Recommended—reliable and quite easy to use:
   - Separate orgasms, with the woman's climax before or after penetration from manual, oral, or other stimulation
   - Simultaneous with the woman stimulating her clitoris during intercourse
   - Simultaneous with the man stimulating the woman's clitoris during intercourse

It's obvious why the first category deserves a negative rating. There is something deeply unfair about sex that is one-sided, and couples are going to be a lot happier if they move away from lovemaking approaches that leave the woman sexually frustrated. When a man and woman make love in a way that's unfulfilling for one partner—virtually always the woman—their sex life tends to wane and become vulnerable to work/life stresses, exhaustion, or arguments. Sex that isn't delivering psychological rewards and a physical payoff to both partners tends to dry up and die.

All the approaches in the second category are attempts to bring the woman to orgasm during intercourse without directly touching the clitoris, and they reportedly work for some couples. But all these techniques are challenging in terms of body positions, timing, and pacing, and there are serious questions about how well they work for most couples over time. Only after much better research is conducted will we know if *any* of them deserve to be moved up to the recommended category.

The third category contains three approaches that are much more straightforward and can work reliably for almost all couples—provided they are willing to put aside the penetration-produces-female-orgasm myth and move beyond standard-issue intercourse. It's impossible to rank-order these approaches because couples tend to have a strong personal preference for one or the other. There is no one best way.

If couples had this kind of consumer guide, most could totally bypass the frustrating (but all too common) choices in the first category. Having access to a comprehensive list of techniques in the second and third categories would help couples avoid stumbling around in the dark and wasting time going up the same blind

> **It's asking a lot of each new generation of lovers to reinvent the wheel and find their way to sexual happiness.**

alleys as their parents and grandparents and great-grandparents before them. It's fun for lovers to be sexually spontaneous and inventive, but each generation shouldn't have to reinvent the whole array of sexual choices.

Given a full menu of options, a couple could explore and find the approach or approaches they liked best. This trial-and-error process is vital, because people don't always know what they want, and an approach that does not tap into authentic personal preferences and doesn't satisfy *both* partners will not stand the test of time. For example, if the woman likes the Hite approach and the man is intensely uncomfortable with it, they should keep looking until they find a better one—or face the fact that they are not sexually compatible, which is a conclusion best reached after six months of exploration rather than after six years of poor communication and avoidance. Of course, tastes and preferences can change, and variety is a good thing, so couples should be willing to keep going back to the menu and keep making new selections as time goes by.

A Design Error?

Let's return to a question posed in Chapter 1: is the placement of the clitoris a design flaw, a slip-up in evolution that makes it far too difficult for humans to have intercourse in ways that please both partners?

There's certainly no escaping the fact that the geography of men's and women's bodies makes mutually satisfying sex a challenge. If we could redesign the human body, would we want to move the clitoris somewhere else? One of the women quoted in *The Hite Report* thought so: "Sex in the best of all possible worlds? My clitoris would be in my vagina, for Christ's sake, so I could come when I fuck!"

But would this work? Sure, the woman's clitoris would be stimulated by her partner's penis during intercourse, but there would still be a problem with pacing and timing. The man's thrusting movements would stimulate the penis and clitoris at the same time and at the same pace, so for lovers to have orgasms together, their timetables would have to be exactly synchronized.

If the man was ahead of his partner on the road to orgasm, he wouldn't be able to slow down his own stimulation without slowing down his partner's, so he would probably end up coming first and leave the woman hanging. An inside-the-vagina clitoris would also make it impossible for the woman to stimulate herself during intercourse. And of course this location for the clitoris would be highly vulnerable to damage during childbirth.

So the fact that the clitoris is a short distance away from the vagina may not be such a bad design after all. It opens up the possibility of simultaneous orgasms for those who like them, since the man—or the woman— can stimulate the clitoris during intercourse.

But taking advantage of this design is neither instinctual nor obvious—and Mother Nature has not provided an instruction manual. Evolution built into the female body the *potential* for orgasms, but not a simple, straightforward mechanism for making them happen during intercourse. Only couples who have excellent sexual rapport and a power-equal relationship can turn the location of the clitoris to their advantage. Through most of human history, this potential has rarely been fulfilled; most of the time, our basic anatomy has skewed sexual intercourse toward male pleasure and female frustration, leaving countless couples without a deep sexual connection.

The question is whether that can change today. We

have a much better understanding of how men's and women's bodies work; there's an increasingly equal division of power between men and women; and sexual communication is improving. But can we reprogram the deeply engrained "Wham, Bam, Thank-You, Ma'am" default setting? Can we make a virtue of the seemingly random way our bodies are designed? Is sexual happiness possible for more than a few lucky couples?

> **Great sex happens when loving couples confront the built-in "geography" challenges of intercourse, explore the full range of techniques, and communicate honestly about what works and doesn't work.**

Sex and Love

Answering these questions really matters. Sex, even though it takes up only a small fraction of our lives, is at the very center of a long-term love relationship—and of our self-esteem, confidence, health, and enjoyment of life. Mutually satisfying sex can bring a couple to new levels of pleasure and happiness. Sex in which both lovers have orgasms promotes monogamy because people who are deeply satisfied with intercourse keep coming back for more. This kind of sex helps people bond and get through the troubles of life. It is the fuel that keeps love burning through the years. It can't save a bad relationship, but for people who really care about one another, it deepens and enriches their love. Great sex truly makes life worth living.

How can we find our way to sexual happiness? It all boils down to the advice a mother might give her daughter as she embarks on her sexual odyssey: "Learn what you like and tell him, honey." Or the advice a father might give his son at the same point in life: "Pay attention. Be patient. No one way solves all. And if she's not happy, you soon won't be either."

Selected Bibliography

These are the books and articles that served as source material for *The Great Sex Secret*. They can add more depth and detail for the interested reader:

Books:

Angier, Natalie. *Woman: An Intimate Geography.* New York, New York: Houghton Mifflin, 1999.

Bell, Ruth, et al. *Changing Bodies, Changing Lives.* New York, New York: Vintage Books, 1988.

Cattrall, Kim and Mark Levinson. *Satisfaction: The Art of the Female Orgasm.* New York, New York: Warner Books, 2002.

Conrad, Sheree and Michael Milburn. *Sexual Intelligence.* New York, New York: Three Rivers Press, 2001.

Davenport, William. *Human Sexuality in Four Perspectives.* Baltimore, Maryland: John Hopkins University Press, 1977.

D'Emilio, John and Estelle Freedman. *Intimate Matters: A History of Sexuality in America.* Chicago, Illinois: University of Chicago Press, 1988, 1997.

Dodson, Betty. *Orgasms for Two: The Joy of Partnersex.* New York, New York: Harmony Books, 2002.

Eichel, Edward and Philip Nobile. *The Perfect Fit: How to Achieve Mutual Fulfillment and Monogamous Passion through the New Intercourse.* New York, New York: Donald I. Fine, 1992.

Fisher, Helen E. *The Sex Contract: The Evolution of Human Behavior.* New York, New York: Quill, 1982.

Freud, Sigmund. Translated and revised by James Strachey. *Three Essays on Sexuality.* New York, New York: Basic Books, 1962.

Hayden, Naura. *How to Satisfy a Woman Every Time…and have her beg for more.* New York, New York: Bibli O'Phile, 1982.

Hite, Shere. *The Hite Report: A Nationwide Study of Female Sexuality.* New York, New York: Macmillan, Dell 1976, 1981.

Hutchins, Claire. *Five Minutes to Orgasm Every Time You Make Love.* Grand Prairie, Texas: JPS Publishing Co., 1998, 2000.

Laqueur, Thomas. *Making Sex: Body and Gender from the Greeks to Freud.* Cambridge, Massachusetts: Harvard University Press, 1990.

Lloyd, Elisabeth A. *The Case of the Female Orgasm: Bias in the Science of Evolution.* Cambridge, Massachusetts: Harvard University Press, 2005.

Maines, Rachel P. *The Technology of Orgasm: "Hysteria," the Vibrator, and Women's Sexual Satisfaction.* Baltimore, Maryland: Johns Hopkins University Press, 1999.

Masters, William H. and Virginia E. Johnson. *Human Sexual Response.* New York, New York: Bantam, 1966.

Boston Women's Health Book Collective. *Our Bodies, Ourselves.* New York, New York: Simon and Schuster, 1971, 1973.

Paget, Lou. *How to Give Her Absolute Pleasure.* New York, New York: Broadway, 2000.

Rhodes, Richard. *Making Love: An Erotic Odyssey.* New York, New York: Simon and Schuster, 1992.

Richardson, Justin and Mark A. Schuster. *Everything You NEVER Wanted Your Kids to Know about SEX (but Were Afraid They'd Ask).* New York, New York: Crown, 2003.

Riskin, Michael and Anita Banker-Riskin with Deborah Grandinetti. *Simultaneous Orgasm and Other Joys of Sexual Intimacy.* Alameda, California: Hunter House, 1997.

Sherfey, Mary Jane. *The Nature and Evolution of Female Sexuality.* New York, New York: Vintage Books, 1966, 1972, 1973.

Silverstein, Judith. Photographs by Jim Jackson.
    Sexual Enhancement for Women. Cambridge,
    Massachusetts: Black and White Publishing
    Company, 1978.

Stoppard, Miriam. *The Magic of Sex.* New York, New
    York: Dorling Kindersley, Inc., 1991, 1992.

Tannahill, Reay. *Sex in History.* Chelsea, Michigan:
    Scarborough House, 1992.

Taylor, Emma and Lorelei Sharkey. *The Big Bang:
    Nerve's Guide to the New Sexual Universe.* New York,
    New York: Plume, 2003.

Taylor, Kate. *The Good Orgasm Guide.* London, Eng-
    land: Simon and Schuster, 2002.

Periodicals:

Byrne, Donn. "A Pregnant Pause in the Sexual Revolution." *Psychology Today,* July 1977.

Deveny, Katheleen. "No Sex, Please, We're Married: Are Stress, Kids and Work Killing Romance?" *Newsweek,* June 30, 2003, 40–46.

Flanagan, Caitlin. "The Wifely Duty." *Atlantic Monthly,* January/February 2003, 171–181.

Johnson, Rebecca. "Sex Advice for the Clinton Age." *New York Times Magazine,* Oct. 4, 1998, 59–61.

Mead, Rebecca. "Love's Labors: Monagamy, Marriage and Other Menaces." *New Yorker*, August 11, 2003.

Trotter, Robert. "The Three Faces of Love: Commitment, Intimacy and Passion Are the Active Ingredients in Sternberg's Three-Sided Theory of Love." *Psychology Today*, September 1986.

Endnotes

Introduction

1 *A widely reported indicator*: Lloyd, 26–37.

Chapter 1: Disappointment in the Land of Eros: Is There a Design Flaw?

8 *More than a decade later*: Johnson, 59.
9 *"A large number of relatively young"*: Flanagan, 171–181.
9 *An infamous issue*: Deveny, 40–46.
11 *no matter how busy life is*: Deveney, 45.
11 *"Embarrassing, isn't it"*: Mead, 82.
12 *"Pity the poor married man"*: Flanagan, 178.
12 *"Marriage remains the most efficient"*: ibid., 181.
14 *A consistent finding of sex research*: Lloyd, 27–39, 112–113. Note that this statistic is for unassisted female orgasms during intercourse. Counting assisted orgasms, the range rises from 31 to 54 percent. Lloyd cites the following sources for her statistics: Terman, 1938; Chesser, 1956; Tavris and Sadd, 1977; Hite,

1976; and Fisher, 1973. She also notes that many studies have not been clear enough in their questions for us to be sure if subjects were talking about assisted or unassisted orgasms and whether the orgasms took place before, during, or after intercourse.

15 *The average adult has*: "National Health and Social Life Survey." *Newsweek*, Oct. 17, 1994, 70.

19 *women need a different kind of stimulation*: Sherfey, 122.

19 *"If you are frightened"*: Angier, 72.

21 *"The first time I had intercourse"*: Bell, 106.

22 *"We rush into it"*: Boston Women's Health Book Collective, 38.

23 *When a woman climaxes*: Fisher, 32.

24 *female orgasm must have an evolutionary*: Lloyd, 220–257.

25 *females' potential for orgasm*: ibid., 107–8.

Chapter 2: Wham, Bam, Thank You, Ma'am: the Long History of One-Sided Sex

29 *"Sex was something that was"*: Boston Women's Health Book Collective, 39.

29 *"We are having intercourse"*: ibid., 37.

30 *sex was an overwhelmingly male-dominated*: Tannahill, 24, 95–98, 146, 286, 423.

30 *"In most of the societies for which"*: Davenport, William. *Human Sexuality in Four Perspectives.*

Baltimore, Maryland: Johns Hopkins University Press, 1977, 115–163.

31 *Nineteenth century, the British surgeon*: Acton, William. *Functions and Disorders of the Reproductive Organs.* Philadelphia, Pennsylvania: Blakiston, 1857, 112.

31 *describe the ignorance of nineteenth-century Americans*: D'Emilio, 5, 19–20.

31 *"It does nothing for me except disgust"*: ibid., 272.

31 *"It was not altogether surprising"*: Tannahill, 354–355.

32 *"I have a sense of guilt"*: D'Emilio, 269.

32 *There was one curious exception*: Tannahill, 119–121.

34 *"the suicidal masturbator"*: ibid., 230.

34 *In the United States*: Kellogg, John Harvey. *Plain Facts for Old and Young.* Burlington, Iowa: I. F. Segner, 1877.

34 *Kellogg believed*: Money, John. *The Destroying Angel.* Amherst, New York: Prometheus Books, 1985.

39 *Women brought up to believe*: ibid., 89–110.

40 *"Dear Madam"*: Eichel, 19.

41 *"It's appalling that men"*: Rhodes, 161.

42 *"Many men don't know how"*: Cattrall, 17–18.

Chapter 3: No Female Orgasm—But He Tried

45 *It is considered a mitzvah*: Edelstein, Amy. "Don't Leave God out of It." *What is Enlightenment?*, Summer/Spring 1998 (Issue #13), 3.

45 *The ancient Chinese Tao sex manuals*: Tannahill, 170.

47 *In 1848, the Bishop of Philadelphia*: Gordella, Peter. *Innocent Ecstasy*. New York, New York: Oxford University Press, 1985.

47 *"those who knew—women—"*: Laqueur, 67.

48 *For more than a thousand years*: Maines, 52, and Laqueur, 9, 49–51, 181–185.

48 *prostitutes did not get pregnant*: Laqueur, 230.

48 *became pregnant after being raped*: Angier, 46.

49 *If she had her orgasm after*: Laqueur, 49–51.

53 *a man isn't born knowing*: Maines, 117.

53 *"Why didn't I just ask her"*: Cattrall, 27.

54 *"Premature ejaculations"*: ibid., 122.

55 *imperviousness to instruction*: Hite, 345–346.

57 *From classical antiquity*: Laqueur, 70–87.

60 *"This time Michael made it"*: Bloom, Judy. *Forever*. New York, New York: Pocket Books, 1975, 149–150.

61 *"an activity engaged in by two"*: Hite, 384.

Chapter 4: Faking It and Dealing with It

63 *that 69 percent of women admitted*: Haze, Delores. "Faking It." *Mademoiselle*, January 1994 (Volume 100, #1), 125.

64 *"true womanliness and femininity"*: Lloyd, 42.

65 *"There is usually some psychological"*: Offit, Avodah Komito. Night *Thought: Reflections of a Sex Therapist.* New York, New York: Congdon & Lattes, Inc, 1981.

68 *like a laboratory animal*: Seeber, Michael, and Carin Gorrell, "The Science of Orgasm: Sex and Your Psyche." *Psychology Today*, November/December 2001, 48–58.

68 *"When I come to the realization"*: Hite, 345–346.

71 *In The Hite Report, 87 percent*: ibid., 420.

72 *"The times when I make love"*: Boston Women's Health Book Collective, 38.

74 *"If the husband should withdraw"*: Eichel, 78–79.

75 *"The clitoris must be wired up"*: Angier, 71.

76 *"When you're young, you masturbate"*: Hite, 385–386.

Chapter 5: Simultaneous Orgasms: Are They Possible?

80 *"In the phallic phase of the girl"*: Freud, Sigmund. *New Introductory Lectures on Psychoanalysis*. New York, New York: Norton, 1933, 161.

80 *Freud even referred one colleague*: Laqueur, 242.

82 *"The clitoris overspills"*: Angier, 75.

83 *Many Victorian medical books*: Angier, 75.

83 *"Freud knew that"*: Laqueur, 233–234.

85 *unilaterally declared that clitoral pleasure*: ibid., 243.

87 *"more like a Rube Goldberg scheme"*: Hite, 275. Hite notes that the analogy may have originated with Dr. Pauline Bart.

90 *"I never have the same sort"*: ibid., 292.

91 *misunderstanding seems to have happened*: Lloyd, 25–26.

93 *In one popular advice book*: D'Emilio, 267.

98 *In the middle of a basic thrust*: Eichel, 165–166.

99 *You realize that you can*: ibid., 168.

100 *In addition, the CAT positions*: ibid., 113.

100 *too difficult, too complicated*: Taylor, 67–68.

102 *Lou Paget has this advice*: Paget, 207.

102 *"the myth of the mutual orgasm"*: Kaplan, Helen Singer. *The New Sex Therapy*. New York, New York: Brunner/Masel, 1981.

102 *"striving to synchronize orgasms*: Stefan Betchell et al. *Sex: A Man's Guide*. New York, New York: Berkley Books, 1998.

103 *last bite at exactly the same*: Michael Castleman. *Sexual Solutions.* New York, New York: Simon and Schuster, 1989.

103 *"I wouldn't want to orgasm"*: http://www.passion-atecommitment.com/faqs/simultaneous.htm#

103 *"We have no idea."*: Taylor and Sharkey, 61.

Chapter 6: Three Approaches to Mutual Satisfaction

108 *new protocol for making love*: D'Emilio, 337.

109 *"Is there anything on this earth"*: Rhodes, 172.

110 *full potential for oral sex*: Kerner, Ian. *She Comes First: A Thinking Man's Guide to Pleasuring a Woman*, New York, New York: Harper Collins, 2004.

112 *One angry guy quoted*: Boston Women's Health Book Collective, 32.

113 *"Most men feel that"*: Lowen, Alexander. *Love and Orgasm.* New York, New York: Macmillan, 1995.

113 *"I have trouble asking"*: Boston Women's Health Book Collective, 38.

115 *"He lost himself to the hilt"*: Updike, John, Couples. New York, New York: Knopf, 1968, 205.

115 *"I was not ever having any"*: Hite, 291.

117 *"In my view, all the intricacies"*: Angier, 69.

117 *"they take responsibility for their pleasure"*: Angier, 70.

120 *cartoon picked up on this feeling*: Smaller, B. Cartoon: "I feel we haven't moved beyond parallel play." *The New Yorker*, May 24, 1999.

120 *Judith Silverstein mentioned this technique*: Silverstein, 66-69.
120 *women who contributed to The Hite Report*: Hite, 293–299.
121 *Only one book in the vast sex literature*: Dodson, 2–3.
124 *"The art of sex"*: Paul. *11 Minutes.* New York, New York: Harper Collins, 2004, 190.
129 *researchers haven't been asking*: Lloyd, 25–26.

Chapter 7: What's Technique Got to Do with It?

135 *Recent accounts of contemporary teenagers*: Denizet-Lewis, Benoit. "Friends, Friends with Benefits and the Benefits of the Local Mall." *New York Times Magazine*, May 30, 2004, 30–58; Flanagan, Caitlin, "Are You There God? It's Me, Monica." *The Atlantic Monthly*, January/February 2006, 167–182.
136 *"The problem with Americans"*: Jong, Erica. "The ZIPless Fallacy," *Newsweek*, June 30, 2003, 48.
138 *"The key to a great sex life"*: Conrad and Milburn, 33.
139 *"OCEAN" personality dimensions*: Wiggins, J.S. *The Five-Factor Model of Personality: Theoretical Perspectives.* New York, New York: Guildford, 1996.
141 *erotophiles and erotophobes*: Byrne, 67–68.
145 *true love can be seen as a triangle*: Trotter, 46–54.
148 *"When sex is good"*: Johnson, 60.
149 *"Most find it easier to have sex"*: Johnson, 61.

150 *shared a telling personal story*: Spencer, Amy. "Turn Her 'No' Into a Go." *Men's Fitness*, July 2003, 62–64.
151 *Respond audibly (not necessarily with words)*: Taylor, K., 52–54.

Chapter 8: Keep Passion Alive in Long-Term Relationships

164 *Most couples settle into a routine*: "The Fodor's Guide to Sex." *The Atlantic Monthly*, January/February 2005, 56.
169 *"your clitoris will always be there"*: Angier, 60.
170 *In the words of Michele Weiner*: Flannagan, 172.
171 *"If you plot the incidence"*: Angier, 199.
172 *nothing sexier these days*: Deveney, 46.
173 *"the kiss is the most compact"*: Taylor and Sharkey, 25.

Chapter 9: Finding Our Way to Sexual Happiness

192 "Sex in the best of all": Hite, 227.